the story of

The Irish Harp

D1611256

CONNACHT
ULSTER
MUNSTER
LEINSTER

DONEGAL

DERRY

ANTRIM

BELFAST

TYRONE
DENBURB

LOUGH NEAGH

DOWN

FERMANAGH

ARMAGH

MONAGHAN

LEITRIM

SLIGO

MAYO

CAVAN

LOUTH

ROSCOMMON

LONG-
FORD

KELLS

MEATH

CAROLAN'S
HOME

WESTMEATH

TARA

GALWAY

OFFALY

DUBLIN

KILDARE

LAOIS

WICKLOW

CLARE

LOUGH
DERG

TIPPERARY

KILKENNY

CARLOW

LIMERICK

ARTHUR
O'NEILL

LIMERICK

WEXFORD

WATERFORD

KERRY

CORK

CORK

KINSALE
1601

B. Konzak ©

✠ CELTIC HIGH CROSSES
- - - BOUNDARY OF PROVINCES
...... COUNTY BOUNDARY
xxx BOUNDARY BETWEEN
REPUBLIC & NORTHERN IRELAND

IRELAND

the story of
The Irish Harp

Its History and Influence

by Nora Joan Clark

North Creek Press

Published by
North Creek Press
P.O. Box 6695
Lynnwood, WA 98036
Book designed and edited by Sylvia Stauffer
Images used in cover illustration by James R. T. Norquay

Editorial assistance by Roberta Wilson, Anna Bezzo-Clark, and Peter Clark
Graphics assistance by Rob Stauffer, Midge Williams, and Emily Johnson
Production assistants: Richard Stauffer and Phoebe Clark

Publisher's – Cataloging in Publication
    (Provided by Quality Books, Inc.)

Clark, Nora Joan
        The story of the Irish harp / Nora Joan Clark — 1st
    ed.
        p. cm.
        Includes bibliographical references and index.
        ISBN 0-9724202-0-7
        1. Celtic harp—Ireland—History. 2. Music—Ireland
    —History and criticism. 3. Musical Instruments—
    Ireland. I. Title.

    ML1015.C3C53 2003   787.9'5

                    QBI02-701977

Library of Congress Control Number: 2002113519

Earlier version of parts of the text of this book originally appeared as a series of four articles published in the American Harp Journal, 1976 to 1970. Used by permission of the American Harp Society

Printed in the United States of America

Foreword

In 1980, I found myself captivated by an unusual instrument. It was a harp — not the large, gilded, ornate instrument found in symphony orchestras, but the small harp, like the one seen on Irish coins (or on the Guinness beer bottle). This magical little instrument was just beginning to make appearances at folk music festivals in the Pacific Northwest and those who fell under its spell had their work cut out for them. I dreamed of being able to play such a harp some day, but in those pre-Internet times, finding resources was not easy.

There were just a handful of recordings which featured the small harp (variously known as Irish, Celtic, or Folk harp), and very few places to find instructional materials, teachers, or anyone who was building these lovely instruments.

I was determined to learn more, though, and investigated every avenue I could think of … and I found that someone else had been down those roads before me. Time after time, I encountered the name of Nora Joan Clark and was told that she knew a lot about the Irish harp, that she owned and played a small harp just like the ones I had been coveting, and that she had been an advocate of this style of harp for decades before I even knew they existed! Her interest in the ethnic harp of Ireland had led her not only to research the subject thoroughly, but also to travel to Ireland, and to meet and correspond with those who were carrying on the tradition of the Irish harp. In this book, Joan now shares the accumulated knowledge of her life-long interest in the Irish harp, and traces its story from the earliest times to the present.

I did eventually find a harp of my own, classes, teachers, and a network of fellow harpers who shared my interest. In the last twenty-five years, folk harps from many cultures, including the Irish harp, have increased in popularity, not just on the west coast of the United States, but throughout the entire country and around the world.

Currently, there are hundreds of harp builders and performers, numerous publications, several large conferences and dozens of regional retreats, and thousands of avocational players all enjoying the delights of this ancient instrument. Those of us who are reaping this bounty now owe a huge debt to those who, like Joan Clark, helped to keep the knowledge alive.

M. Diane Moss
Shoreline, Washington
July 2003

In Memory of the Life and Music of
Derek Fleetwood Bell
1935 — 2002

Introduction

FIGURE 1. CROSS OF MUIREDACH IN ITS SETTING AT THE ABBEY OF MONASTERBOICE, COUNTY LOUTH, IRELAND. EIGHTEEN-FOOT TALL STONE CROSS, CIRCA 922 AD.

The old Irish harp is derived from harps that have been used for centuries by the peoples of Ireland and nearby Celtic-language lands such as Scotland, Wales, and Brittany. Carved in stone on early Celtic crosses is evidence of triangular harps being played in the first century A.D., perhaps even earlier. Metal strings were customary on the sturdy ancient Irish harps, which were played with the fingernails. These harps were small, two to four feet in height, and easily carried about.

Around the end of the 18th century, due to historical and cultural changes, the nail technique of playing on stout harps with wire strings nearly died out. Adopting the curved body form and refined lines of the early European pedal harps, the Irish harps of the 19th and early 20th century, more properly known as neo-Irish harps, were generally strung with gut, and later nylon was used.

In recent years, the term "Irish harp" is undergoing some redefinition, with a wide array of styles now in use, the most remarkable of which may be the use of the nails again to play upon wire-strung harps.

* * * *

The art of the ancient Irish harper was part of a long-lasting oral tradition of which we have no written record other than the admiring descriptions by contemporary historians in prior centuries. Although the ancient poetry came to be preserved in writing, the music that accompanied the words was never set down in any identifiable form. Retained in the mind of the artist, the music was as secure as the position of the harper in flourishing times. When Ireland fell under foreign dominion, however, its early culture gradually eroded and almost faded out, either through neglect or by deliberate design. The old bardic order, with its emphasis on language, poetics, and musical training, declined over time, in some places totally abandonded, in others faded and changed. Amid invasions and oppressions, the early harp music of Ireland was lost.

During the period of Turlough O'Carolan, the great harper-composer (1670-1738), it was still not the practice to write music down. The music by which Carolan made his living was created in the bardic oral tradition and committed to memory. In spite of the strenuous work of collectors such as Edward Bunting, who produced an invaluable collection of the music of Irish harpers in the late 18th and early 19th centuries, little exists in print that provides contemporary harpists with accurate examples of the technique or style of the old harpers.

By the 19th century, the Irish harp was threatened with extinction. The suffering conditions of Ireland and the massive migrations that began about mid-century, along with the rising use of the pedal harp and piano by those who could afford them, provided for little interest in an old instrument. And not just the harp, but more seriously, the Gaelic language that had been spoken for centuries was in danger of dying out.

The Gaelic revival of the late 19th and early 20th centuries and the rediscovery of Gaelic literature though the artistic efforts of W.B. Yeats and others contributed to a new mood of nationalistic idealism. The image of the historical Trinity College Harp, used as early as the 15th century on coins in Ireland by conquering monarchs, was reinstated in the 1920s to grace the coins of the emerging nation.

✳ ✳ ✳ ✳

Obscure in the midst of that ferment was the position of the Irish harp in Ireland. The music and traditional methods of playing this harp were preserved, in part, by Catholic nuns in the security of the convent. In 1903, an excellent study, *Tutor for the Irish Harp*, was authored by Sister M. Attracta Coffey of Loreto Abbey, Rathfarnham, Dublin.

In the year 1900, my mother, a ten-year old schoolgirl at the time, heard Sister Attracta play for her majesty Queen Victoria on the occasion of the monarch's visit to Loreto Abbey. Although dimmed with age, my mother's eyes glowed with pride as she would retell the story of how she had heard Sister Attracta play the harp. With straightened back and quavering voice, Norah, daughter of O'Donnell, would relive the moment when the plucky Irish nun played "Go Where Glory Waits Thee!" for the aged British queen.

✷ ✷ ✷ ✷

Over the years, partly from the influence of my Irish background, and partly from a simple love of the music, I have played and been interested in harps and harp music, the Irish harp in particular. During my travels to Ireland and elsewhere, I have had the privilege of meeting a number of the musicians mentioned in this book. From the time I began my study of the Irish harp in the 1970s, to the present day, I have seen an astonishing array of what we used to call simply the Irish harp, now branched and developed into many forms.

A number of independent craftspeople around the world started making small harps in the 1970s, leading to a wide variety of what came to be known as "folk harps." Such efforts by various harpmakers became established by the 1980s and grew to wide distribution and use in the 1990s. When considering the harp scene of today, certainly there are many influences other than that of the Irish harp, especially in the United States. The story of the Irish harp is one thread in the history of the small harps we see today, including what are called Celtic, Gaelic, and Folk harps. Others have written and will continue to write about this great variety of harps, whose only similarity may be that they do not have pedals and are small enough to be carried about by the player.

What we see today builds upon what has come before — that is, the ancient bards, the medieval harpers, the early harpmakers, the classical harpists, and the musical, cultural, and political revivals of one kind and another through the centuries.

In offering this book based on my understanding and point of view, I hope to help my readers become more aware of the rich history associated with the harp of Ireland, and to see how its influence has spread and grown. In Ireland, certainly, there is a strong tradition being carried on and moved forward in the work of contemporary harpmakers and musicians. In countries close to Ireland, as well, there is much activity with variations of the small harp. And from my perspective, in the northwest corner of the United States, I find that the influence of the Irish harp, along with a growing interest in small harps of all styles and origins, to be a fascinating development.

Chaper 1
Celtic Origins
of the Irish Harp
From the 3rd Century BC

Chaper 1 ~ Celtic Origins of the Irish Harp
From the 3rd Century BC

Early Events in Celtic History

c. 1100 B.C.   *Celtic peoples identified in Central Europe*

c. 800 B.C.   *Celts driven westward toward western edge of Europe*

Fourth Century BC

c. 400 B.C.   *Evidence of Celtic civilization in present-day Ireland*

AD Fifth and Sixth Centuries

c. A.D. 500   *Migration of Celtic peoples from Ireland to Scotland*

A.D. 563   *St.Columcille founds monestary at Iona*

Through the ages the harp has been associated with the Celtic peoples, a loose federation of European tribes defined and united by language and custom, inhabiting parts of the British Isles and the west coast of France. The origin of what is known as the Irish harp is somewhat obscure but there is general agreement that the Irish harp is, with certain variations, a musical instrument representative of all the Celtic peoples. As Joan Rimmer points out in *The Irish Harp*: "It seems highly probable that the characteristic stringed instrument of the Celts was a U-shaped lyre, originating … in South-west Asia. It seems, too, that the Celts may have preserved it in something not far removed from its original form for a thousand years or so."[1]

Celtic peoples have been identified as early as the twelfth century B.C. in the area that is now southwest Germany and eastern France. Under pressure from the Germanic Teutons, who had been penetrating westward ever since the eighth century B.C., the Celts were driven west from the Near East to the edge of Europe, moving north to settle in the British Isles and south to what is now the Iberian Peninsula in Spain. The Celts were a fierce fighting people, who invaded many lands and became known throughout Europe. The Celtic incursions included the Greek world and the area in present-day Turkey known as Galatia.

As early as the third century B.C., archaeological records identify evidence of the Celts in Ireland. Proinsias MacCana, a prominent Irish scholar, begins his book *Celtic Mythology* with this description of the Celts:

> The unity of the Celts of antiquity was one of culture rather than of race. Those peoples whom the Greeks and Romans

knew as Celts no doubt were sprung from various ethnic origins, but in the view of external observers, they had sufficient shared features — in language and nomenclature, social and political institutions, and in general their way of life — to mark them off as a recognizably distinct nation.[2]

Celtic people never formed a strong centralized government or political empire, and have been noted more for gifts of imagination and an affinity for the irrational than for the political arts of organization. MacCana mentions some attributes that have been applied to the Celtic character over the centuries, and which persist in popular notions, namely the Celtic "eloquence, lyric genius, volatile temperament, prodigality, reckless bravery, ebullience, contentiousness, and so on ... ." It is likely this view of the Celts is not merely mythical, MacCana states, but has persisted due to its accuracy.

Poetic and musical inclination are deeply rooted in a rich oral tradition supported by custom, such as existed among the Celts. Though less known for physical arts such as architecture, sculpture, and representative painting, Celtic influence upon Western civilization has been considerable through its hold upon the mind and the spirit.

* * * *

Ancient Celtic peoples inhabited and flourished in six distinct areas, sometimes referred to as the Pan-Celtic Nations and defined by the development of language. There were two branches of the Celtic language and peoples. The northern, or *Goidelic* branch, occupied what is now Ireland, Scotland, and the Isle of Man. The southern, or *Brithonic* branch, resided in the areas of present-day Wales, Cornwall, and Brittany. In Ireland and Scotland today, versions of the old Gaelic languages are still spoken: in Ireland as "Gaelic," or "Irish," and in Scotland as "Scotts Gaelic." Until mid-twentieth century, Manx, the language of the Isle of Man, was still spoken just as in Brittany people still spoke Breton, a language closely related to Welsh, still flourishing in the bilingual country of Wales.

FIGURE 2. THE SIX PAN-CELTIC NATIONS HAVE CELTIC LANGUAGE ROOTS: IRELAND, SCOTLAND, ISLE OF MAN, WALES, CORNWALL, AND BRITTANY.

Also related to Welsh is Cornish, the language of the Cornish Peninsula, which along with the Breton language is enjoying a recent revival.

* * * *

It is intriguing to trace the migrations of these varied Celtic peoples, their trade as well as their wars, and their similarities and differences not only in language but also in music. For example, the harp has been particularly important in the cultural history of Wales, descending from Welsh Druidic society and stimulated by Irish influence. Along with other musical and poetic arts, the harp was perpetuated in Wales by historic festivals known as Eisteddfod, cultural performances that are still held today.

The Celtic peoples of Brittany also have a special attachment to the harp, with their language and music having a unique character due to their proximity to France. The harp may have been brought to Brittany during the time when Celtic

Bretons migrated from what is now the south of England to Brittany. An early innovator in the revival of the Celtic harp in Brittany, Jord Cochevelou, comments on how the harp came to his region in France: "As early as the fifth century, Irish missionaries come to convert the Isle of Britain were in the habit of accompanying their psalms with a little harp...." Cochevelou also mentions various medieval harps derived from the Irish harp that appear in stained glass, tapestries, and paintings throughout Europe. He surmises that, although this harp of Irish roots was abandoned along with the Breton language and culture around the fifteenth century, the ancient harp "was to remain alive in memory, ever more beautiful and evocative, perhaps because of having become exclusively a symbol of art, poetry, grace, purity and enchantment...."[3]

Migrating north in the sixth century A.D., across the sea to what is now Scotland, ancient Celtic peoples from the island then known as "Scotia" brought with them their name. There is good evidence that the triangular harp may have originated in Scotland, rather than in Ireland. However, the peoples from Scotia (now Ireland) brought their knowledge of music and the arts along with them. One of these travelers, St. Columba, widely known in Ireland as St. Columcille, founded a monastery in the year A.D. 563 at Iona, a tiny island of the inner Hebrides on the west coast of Scotland. St. Columcille, also known as the "Dove," was himself a poet as well as a priest, and is best known for his work as founder of the exquisite record of the gospels created at Iona, the Book of Kells. As a patron of the Irish poets, St. Columcille fostered both the musical and the literary arts; some of his fellow monastics may have accompanied their hymns with music on the harp.

From the work of the monastery at Iona, Christianity spread throughout Scotland and with it spread the influence of the arts, including music and perhaps some harp playing in the style of the ancient harpers.

Chapter 2
Glimpses
of the Ancient Harp
In Ireland, the 9th to 15th Centuries

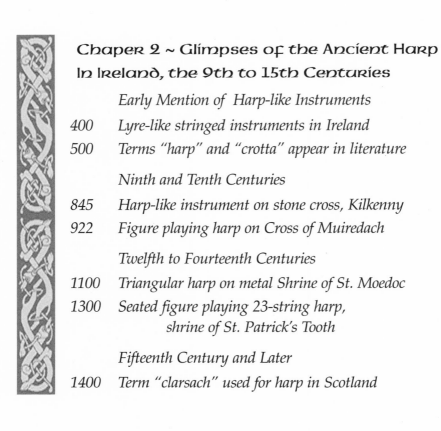

Chaper 2 ~ Glimpses of the Ancient Harp In Ireland, the 9th to 15th Centuries

Early Mention of Harp-like Instruments

400   *Lyre-like stringed instruments in Ireland*

500   *Terms "harp" and "crotta" appear in literature*

Ninth and Tenth Centuries

845   *Harp-like instrument on stone cross, Kilkenny*

922   *Figure playing harp on Cross of Muiredach*

Twelfth to Fourteenth Centuries

1100   *Triangular harp on metal Shrine of St. Moedoc*

1300   *Seated figure playing 23-string harp,*
           shrine of St. Patrick's Tooth

Fifteenth Century and Later

1400   *Term "clarsach" used for harp in Scotland*

Stringed instruments used in pre-Christian Ireland long before any type of harp was known in that part of the world were variations of the lyre. While a lyre is basically a U-shaped frame with strings, a "harp" can be defined as being triangular, with some sort of soundbox, a neck, a post, and strings of graded length. Over time, use of the harp displaced that of the lyre in Ireland.

One account of the ancient harp of Ireland written near the end of the sixteenth century shows how the harp was viewed from an Italian perspective. In his *Dialogue on Ancient and Modern Music* published in Florence in 1581, Vincenzo Galilei writes:

> Among the stringed instruments now in use in Italy, the first is the Harp, which is only an ancient cithara, so far altered in form by the artificers of those days as to adapt it to the additional number, and the tension of the strings, containing from the highest to the lowest note, more than three octaves.

> This most ancient instrument was brought to us from Ireland (as Dante says) where they are excellently made, and in great numbers, the inhabitants of that island having practiced on it for many and many ages; nay, they even place it in the arms of the kingdom, and paint it on their public buildings, and stamp it on their coin, giving as the reason their being descended from the royal prophet David. [4]

The exact origin of the triangular, frame harp of the Celts is not entirely known, but the subject has been explored in depth in several excellent books. Joan Rimmer, in *The Irish Harp* (1967) suggests that the triangular form of Celtic harps that were known in ancient Ireland may have been a transformation or adaptation of similar instruments used in early Near-Eastern cultures. Building on Rimmer's information and other research, the history of the Celtic harp is further explored by Keith Sanger and Allison Kinnard in their book *Tree of*

Strings (1992). A comprehensive history of the harp in Scotland, this book provides evidence that the triangular-framed harp appeared in Scotland much earlier than it did in Ireland.

The earliest representations of a harp-like form in Ireland are those carved in stone on monumental High Crosses that date from the ninth and tenth centuries. Erected in Celtic countries as religious monuments, these massive structures have the characteristic Celtic circle spanning the arms of the cross. Some stone crosses were elaborately carved with scenes from the Old and New Testament, and several of these portray musicians with instruments that are clearly early harps.

HARP-LIKE INSTRUMENTS ON 9TH CENTURY CROSSES

AD 845 Harp on Ullard Cross

Of the several examples of harp-like instruments of rectangular form found in Ireland, one famous image is on the Ullard Cross in County Kilkenny, dating from about A.D. 845. On the left arm of this cross, a seated figure playing a harp-like instrument of rectangular form is sculpted into the stone.

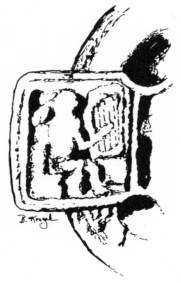

FIGURE 3. HARP-LIKE INSTRUMENT OF RECTANGULAR FORM CARVED ON ULLARD CROSS, COUNTY KILKENNY, IRELAND, STONE CROSS, CIRCA 845 A.D.

FIGURE 4. ANCIENT MUSICIAN PLAYING HARP-LIKE INSTRUMENT. STONE CARVING, NORTH CROSS AT CASTLEDERMOT, COUNTY KILDARE, IRELAND. FROM THE 9TH CENTURY.

The harp is held on the knee of the musician, and appears to have had six strings. While the exact form of the harp on the Ullard Cross is unclear, it remains a valuable image that shows the size of the instrument with respect to the performer and the playing position.

AD 800 Harp player on North Cross

Another example of a figure playing an upright stringed instrument held in the lap, with arms raised to pluck the strings, is found on the North Cross at Castledermot (figure 4). In this photo, though the image is highly eroded, five or six strings are visible, and the position of the figure in the chair is similar to that of the Ullard Cross. As Joan Rimmer notes, an interesting apect of the harps on Irish crosses is that they are all shown being played. [5]

27

FIGURE 5. DETAIL FROM THE CROSS OF MUIREDACH, SCENE OF THE LAST JUDGEMENT WITH CHRIST FIGURE AT CENTER. FIGURE PLAYING HARP TO THE RIGHT OF CENTRAL FIGURE. COUNTY LOUTH, IRELAND, CIRCA A.D. 922.

EARLY HARP ON THE CROSS OF MUIREDACH

Cross of Muiredach, A.D. 922

Perhaps the most splendid of all the Irish sculptured crosses is the Cross of Muiredach, which can be seen today at the historical Abbey of Monasterboice, County Louth. The central circle of this eighteen-foot monument depicts scenes from the Last Judgement, with the figure of Christ holding a cross and scepter. On the east-facing side of the cross, to the left side of the Christ figure, a musician is playing a wind instrument. To the right of the Christ, a seated figure is playing what appears to be a triangular harp (figure 5).

Whether this figure in fact represents a true triangular frame harp or not is unclear. However, the shape of the harp on this High Cross is a marked contrast to the earlier rounded or quadrangular forms like those seen on the Ullard Cross and the North Cross at Casteldermot, which are more closely related to the lyre.

TRIANGULAR HARP, SHRINE OF ST. MOEDOC

St. Moedoc Shrine, c. 1100.

An early example in Ireland of a harp that is clearly triangular is found on the 11th century metal shrine of St. Moedoc. The cast bronze reliquary has a triangular-shaped upper structure fitted with a plaque or door, mounted by a heavy ring. The plaque is embellished with a carving of a seated, bearded figure in flowing robes playing a harp, which rests on the knees of the player and leans against his left shoulder. Eight or nine strings are visible and are plucked by the fingers of the right

FIGURE 6. TRIANGULAR HARP ON SHRINE OF ST. MOEDOC. FIGURE IN FLOWING ROBES PLAYING A TRIANGULAR HARP, WITH LARGE BIRD PERCHED ON TOP. CAST BRONZE RELIQUARY, CIRCA A.D. 1100.

FIGURE 7. DETAIL FROM DRAWING OF THE HARP PLAYER ON ST. MOEDOC SHRINE.

hand in the bass while the left hand is barely visible behind the strings in the treble. Perched atop the harp is the image of a large bird.

MEDIEVAL HARP, SHRINE OF ST. PATRICK'S TOOTH,

The 14th century Shrine of St. Patrick's Tooth (figure 8), so named because it is believed to have contained a relic of the venerable saint, is decorated with carving that shows a medieval harp somewhat larger than that of St. Moedoc's Shrine, having approximately twenty-three strings. The triangular harp with curved forepillar is balanced against the player's knees and left shoulder. It is being played with the left hand in the treble and the right hand in the bass.

St. Patrick shrine, c. 1300.

Both the St. Moedoc and St. Patrick shrines can be viewed today at the National Museum of Ireland in Dublin.

GAELIC LANGUAGE NAMES FOR THE HARP

"Harp" appears in Roman literature 6th century

In the sixth century A.D., the term "harp" appeared in literature, in the lines of a poem by the well known Roman bishop Venantius Fortunatus, Bishop of Poitiers. Here are the lines from the Latin, followed by a translation provided by Joan Rimmer:

> *Romanus lyra, plaudat tibi barbarus harpa,*
> *Græcus Achilliaca, crotta Brttanna canat.*
>
> The Romans praise thee with the lyre,
> The barbarians with the harp,
> The Greeks with the Achillean lyre,
> The Britons with the crotta. [6]

It is interesting to note that, in these lines from the sixth century, distinctions are made between several types of plucked stringed instruments. Romans played the lyre, while the "barbarians" (Teutonic peoples) use a "harp," although *harp* as used here may have been just another name for a form of lyre. The Greeks had their particular form, the Achillean lyre, while the Celtic Britons used the *crotta*. The term, *crotta*, is related to the old Irish word for harp, *cruit*, which originally meant simply a stringed instrument, or lyre. As the harp gradually displaced the use of the lyre, the terms *crotta* or *cruit* came to refer specifically to the harp. In 1905, W. H. Grattan Flood, an Irish historian, refers to an unnamed Irish poet from fourth century B.C., and offers an explanation of the terms:

> The old Irish name for the harp was *crott* or *cruit*. Originally a small instrument of three or four strings, plucked with the fingers, it is mentioned by an Irish poet who flourished about four hundred years before Christ. Subsequently this Irish cruit was played with a plectrum, or bow…the *chrotta* was a small harp played with a bow, generally placed resting on the knees, or on a table before the performer. [7]

In contrast to the *cruit*, or small ancient harp, the harp of medieval Ireland was a larger instrument of some thirty strings, known as the *clairsech*, or *cláirseach*. From the late 15th

FIGURE 8. SEATED FIGURE PLAYING TRIANGU-
LAR HARP OF ABOUT TWENTY-THREE STRINGS.
METAL SHRINE OF ST. PATRICK'S TOOTH.
CIRCA A.D. 1300.

century in Scotland, and from the 16th century in Ireland, the
term *clársach*, was used to refer to the harp, in addition to the
older word, *cruit*.

Evidence that some form of harp was known in all the
Celtic lands is shown by the fact that each of the Pan-Celtic
languages have a distinct term specifically for this instrument.
The word "harp" can be translated as *telenn* in Breton, *telyn* in
the related Welsh language, as well as *clársaich* or *cláirseach* in
the Irish, and *clàrsach* in the closely related Scotts Gaelic.

IMPORTANCE OF MUSIC IN THE LIFE OF THE ANCIENTS

Frequent references to the art of music in early medieval manuscripts demonstrate the importance of music in the life of the
ancients. Music-making at banquets and ceremonious occasions is often described, with music used for magical purposes
as well as inciting warriors to battle.

Specific accounts of harps and harpers occur in medieval
Celtic legends such as the tales of King Arthur and his Knights
of the Round Table. In Sir Thomas Malory's fifteenth century

version of this legend, *Le Morte d'Artur*, we meet Tristan as a harper. Young Tristan, a prince of Cornwall, was sent to France, as the story goes:

> "...to learn the language, and nurture and deeds of arms.... And there was Tristan more than seven years.... And so Tristan learned to be an harper passing all other, that there was none such called in no country, and so in harping and on instruments of music he applied him in his youth for to learn."[8]

15th century Harper in King Arthur legend

Young Tristan took his harp with him and sailed to Ireland in the service of King Mark of Cornwall. Arriving in Ireland he was warmly welcomed for his skill as a harper, and here it was that he met his love, the Princess Isolde, whom he taught to play the harp.

Tristan was eventually slain by the jealous King Mark "as he sat harping before his lady, La Belle Isolde." Sir Malory's early version of this great love tragedy might appeal to the harpist more than Wagner's later realization in his famous opera, *Tristan and Isolde*; in Malory's account it seems that instead of a love potion, the tragic pair were enchanted by music of the harp.

GIRALDUS CAMBRENSIS DESCRIBES IRISH MUSIC

1182 Cambrensis writes of Irish music

More on the romantic aspects of Irish music is found in one of the most often quoted passages on the subject of music in medieval Ireland. In the year 1183, Giraldus Cambrensis, a Welsh-born churchman and historian, journed to Ireland as chaplain to Prince John, son of King Henry II of England. Ireland was subject to the rule of Anglo-Norman authority at the time, and King Henry had sent his son John to govern the conquered island. As a result of this journey, Cambrensis wrote his famous account of Ireland, *Topographia Hibernica*.

Cambrensis wrote in the Welsh language of his time. The following translation is provided by Edward Bunting, in the preface to his book, *A General Collection of the Ancient Irish Music* (1796). The famous description is glowing in its detail:

> The attention of this people to Musical Instruments I find worthy of commendation; in which their skill is, beyond all comparison superior to any Nation I have ever seen: for in these the modulation is not slow and solemn, as in the Instruments of Britain, to which we are accustomed; but the sounds are rapid and precipitate, yet at the same time sweet and pleasing.

After commenting on the extreme musical excellence of the Irish, Cambrensis continues his preface remarks with an enthusiastic description of the harpers he heard in twelfth century Ireland:

> It is wonderful how in such precipitate rapidity of the fingers the Musical proportions are preserved; and by their art faultless throughout, in the midst of their complicated modulation and most intricate arrangement of notes by a rapidity so sweet, a regularity so irregular, a concord so discordant, the melody is rendered harmonious and perfect: whether the chord of the Diatesseron [the fourth] or Diapente [the fifth] are struck together, yet they always begin in a soft mood, and end in the same, that all may be perfected in the sweetness of delicious sounds.
>
> They enter on, and again leave their modulations with so much subtlety, and the tinglings of the small strings sport with so much freedom under the deep notes of the Bass, delight with so much delicacy, and sooth so softly that the excellence of their art seems to lie in concealing it. [9]

It is not so surprising that this observer took note of Irish music. The skills of these musicians may have taken twenty years of special training to perfect in the traditional Bardic schools.

Chapter 3
Harpers, Druids,
and the Bardic Tradition
From Ancient Times to the 17th Century

Chaper 3~ Harpers, Druids, & the Bardic Tradition
From Ancient Times to the 17th Century

Fourth Century BC

c. 400 BC   Ancient druids and bards in Celtic lands

AD Fourth and Fifth Centuries

350   Height of ancient society at Tara, seat of High Kings
432   St. Patrick arrives in Ireland

Sixth Century

c. 500   Druidic learned class, harpers and bards perform
*   the Suantraighe, Goltraighe, and Geantraighe*
560   Last great Feis of Tara
564   St. Columcille in exile from Ireland, goes to Iona

Ninth to Seventeenth Centuries

800 to 1000   Viking invasions of Ireland
1200 to 1300   Anglo-Norman conquest of Ireland
1400 to 1700   Gaelic civilization, with bardic influences
*   flourishes and continues in Ireland*

*c. 400 B.C.
Ancient
druids and
bards in
Celtic lands*

The so-called pagans of pre-Christian Ireland had a highly developed society, presided over by the *druids*, who ranked next in importance to the kings. As early as the fourth century B.C., druids were the learned class, the priests and lawgivers, with important civil functions and privileges. The druids were also the poets. As Donal O'Sullivan points out in *Carolan, The Life Times and Music of an Irish Harper*, the poets had a special place in society:

> This Gaelic civilization had its annalists, its compilers of legal codes and other writers of prose, but the predominant literary influence from a cultural point of view was exercised by the court poets who were the product of the bardic schools....They were members of an hereditary profession, who were accorded a superior social status and who had received a thorough training in all that appertained to their career. [10]

Druids also served as physicians and teachers, maintaining an elaborate system for the education of their ranks, an oral tradition that required as much as twenty years of training. During this time the function of the poet and that of the harp player were distinct, but it is probable that the harper received equivalent training. It is known that the position of the harper was highly honored and next only to that of the chief poet.

Eugene O'Curry, a renowned scholar and lecturer on ancient Irish history, writing in 1873, mentions the importance of the harp and of musicians in the traditions of Ireland:

> In no country in Europe, at least I believe so, is the antiquity and influence of the harp thrown back into the darker regions of history as in Érinn.... It is, indeed a remote tradition; but it is identified with a people and with persons whose history, though obscure and exaggerated, is still embodied in our oldest chronicles, and has never departed from the memories of

our living romances and popular traditions. And, from the
very remotest period ... we find music, musical instruments,
musical performers, and the power and influence of music
spoken of. [11]

The File, the Bard, and the Harper

Three distinct artistic classes were associated with the bardic
tradition of drudic society: the poet, the bard, and the harper.
The highest ranking of the three, the poet or *file*, composed
heroic poetry in praise of his hosts, the lords and kings. Such
works created by the *file* also preserved the history and laws
of the land. Of lesser rank was the bard, or *reacaire*, whose
duty it was to recite the compositions of the poet on ceremo-
nial occasions to the accompaniment of stringed instruments.
The role of the harper, close in rank to that of the poet, was to
accompany the recitation with the harp, and to be extremely
proficient at this difficult instrument.

The harpers and other musicians were highly educated
and enjoyed the special privileges extended to the poets. In
addition to their elevated status, mystical powers were attributed to their instruments and bardic performers were both
venerated and feared. In an article titled "The Oracular Nature of the Early Celtic Harp," one scholar discusses the harp
as an instrument for divination, with magical powers that inspired mystical messages. Oak and willow were primarily
used for traditional construction of Irish harps, although maple
would have been more durable, possibly due to the mytho-
logical sacred nature of these trees. Druidic ceremonies were
performed in oak groves, with the great sacred trees an
important symbol of the security and integrity of the tribal
kings. [12] A mystical veneration of the sound of the harp still
exists today, which harkens back to what may have been experienced by the ancient musicians.

Suantraighe, Goltraighe, and Geantraighe

The harp was played, in ancient Ireland, not only as accompaniment to the poets, but also as a solo instrument. Harpers were expected to be able to influence the moods of the company with their music. In his remarkable book, *The Irish and The Highland Harps*, Robert Bruce Armstrong provides a comprehensive history of the Irish harp and its place in the ancient society. Armstrong includes this quotation from Eugene O'Curry, explaining the situation.

> The Ollamhs [professors] of Music, or those raised to the highest order of Musicians of ancient Érinn, were obliged by the rules of the order to be perfectly accomplished in the performance of three peculiar classes or pieces of music, namely the *Suantraighe*, which no one could hear without falling into a delightful slumber; the *Goltraighe*, which no one could hear without bursting into tears and lamentations; and the *Geantraighe*, which no one could hear without bursting out into loud and irrepressible laughter.[13]

These three themes, the slumber music, the lament, and the joyful piece, appear again and again in works of music with Irish influence over the centuries.

Harps at Tara, the Seat of High Kings

A.D. 200 - 300 Height of Tara and High Kings

Much ancient music and bardic verse was certainly heard at Tara, the seat of High Kings in old Ireland. From prehistoric times, possibly as early as 400 B.C., until the sixth century A.D., Tara was the religious, political, and cultural capital of Ireland. The site of Tara is a low hill commanding an extensive view over the central plains of Ireland in County Meath.

Tara reached the height of its glory in the third century A.D., when under the rule of King Cormac MacArt, a large complex of buildings was situated on or around the hill. Every three years the *Feis of Tara* would be held for six days, starting the third day before the feast of *Samhain*, which is also known as All-Hallowtide (the first of November). This event was a joint legislative and cultural assembly, marking and celebrating kingships, weddings, and other important events. When the business of the day was concluded there was poetry, music, and minstrelsy in the banquet hall.

The last great *Feis of Tara* was held in A.D. 560 under the reign of King Dermot MacFergus . The ending of this tradition may mark the final Christianization of the Tara monarchy. Today, nothing remains of Tara but a ring-shaped mound atop the hill.

AD 560 Last great Feis of Tara

Centuries later, to arouse his countrymen's spirit during their suppression by the English, the fall of Tara was memorialized in 1807 by the 19th century Irish poet, Thomas Moore. Because the poem captures so well the spirit of what Tara was, or might have been, the entire poem is included here. [14]

The Harp That Once Thro' Tara's Halls

by Thomas Moore

The harp that once thro' Tara's halls
    The soul of music shed
Now hangs as mute on Tara's walls
    As if that soul were fled –
So sleeps the pride of former days,
    So glory's thrill is o'er,
And hearts, that once beat high for praise,
    Now feel that pulse no more.

No more to chiefs and ladies bright
    The harp of Tara swells;
The chord alone, that breaks at night,
    Its tale of ruin tells.
Thus Freedom now so seldom wakes,
    The only throb she gives,
Is when some heart indignant breaks,
    To show that still she lives.

INFLUENCE OF THE BARDIC SCHOOLS IN IRELAND

c. 500 - 600
Christians
displace the
druids

Although Christian missionaries displaced the druids in the 5th and 6th centuries A.D., the learned traditions of the bardic order continued. Christian ecclesiastics adopted the harp and may have sung psalms and hymns accompanied by the *cruit*, or small harp. In addition, a unique aspect of the history of Ireland is that unlike most of the rest of Europe, this island nation was never invaded or colonized by the Romans.

THE CELTIC FRINGE, UNTOUCHED BY ROMAN CONQUEST

The significance of this history is explored in depth by Thomas Cahill in his 1995 bestseller, *How the Irish Saved Civilization, The Untold Story of Ireland's Heroic Role from the Fall of Rome to the Rise of Medieval Europe*. In the book, Cahill tells how the tradition of scholarship among the Irish and the copying of texts by the monastics prevented the demise of a good portion of the great literature of the time, as Europe sank into the Dark Ages. Cahill describes the situation in the 6th century: "Ireland, at peace and furiously copying, thus stood in the position of becoming Europe's publisher.... While Rome and its ancient empire faded from memory and a new, illiterate Europe rose on its ruins, a vibrant, literary culture was blooming in secret along its Celtic fringe." [15]

564
Saint
Columcille
in exile
to Iona

Cahill includes a detailed description of the importance of St. Columcille. Exiled from Ireland in A.D. 564 to the monastery at Iona (an island off Scotland), this saint took learning and literature back to the barbarized land. One incident shows Columcille defending the bards on a rare return visit to Ireland in the presence of the authorities of an Irish kingdom:

> Also on the agenda was a proposal to suppress the order of the bards, admittedly a troublesome lot, whose satires were potent enough to kill and who took the most presumptuous advantage wherever they happened to camp. Poetry, said

Columuncille (who was himself the most accomplished poet of his day) was an essential part of Irish life: Ireland could not be Ireland without it. [16]

CELTIC AND CHRISTIAN CULTURES MERGE IN GAELIC SOCIETY

The lack of Roman influence in Ireland allowed the Celtic culture and way of life to persist well into medieval times. When St. Patrick arrived in 5th century Ireland, two insular traditions, that of the druids, and the Christians were merged. Early Christians in Ireland tolerated and adapted their rituals to pagan rites and practices. As Proinsias MacCana states in *Celtic Mythology* (1970): "It is also significant that so many pagan traditions and cults survived and flourished almost to our own day in consequence of the fact that they were accommodated under the capacious mantle of the Church and thereby acquired a rather spurious seal of respectability." [17]

In spite of the Viking invasions of Ireland in the 9th to 11th centuries and the Anglo-Norman conquest, which began in the 12th century, the learned druidic traditions and bardic schools continued for centuries. Although many attempts were made by various invaders to suppress or eliminate traditional Irish culture, Gaelic civilization flourished practically unchanged in Ireland up until the end of the 15th century.

800 to 1000 Viking invasions of Ireland

In *The Hidden Ireland*, a book about the life of the 18th century Irish peasant as shown through literature, Daniel Corkery comments on the importance of the bardic schools in the life of the Irish, and traces the history of these influential traditions. He points out that the bardic institutions were run by laymen and existed in parallel with the clerical schools. What the bards offered was most important to the Irish: "Irish civilization was from the beginning marked by intellectual passion. Now, the bardic schools were the seat of that passion." [18] In another passage, Corkery comments on the mingling of pagan and Christian cultures:

> It is not probable that we shall ever discover the origins of the bardic schools. They were ancient when St. Patrick came amongst us. In the pagan days poet and druid were perhaps one; and even after those schools had become Christian some vestiges of the old cult still survived in them; but this, of course, could naturally be said of life in general, for pagan ways of thinking, pagan traditions and customs, lingered on through whole centuries. [19]

The influence of the poets was enormous in shaping and perpetuating the Gaelic language and the ideas, feelings, and knowledge transmitted by that language.

Big House and Cabin, a Shared Culture

1200 to 1300, Anglo-Norman presence in Ireland

During the Middle Ages, Ireland was composed of a rural Gaelic-speaking society dominated by aristocratic Celtic families and the monastic presence of Christianity. At the same time, the English-speaking Anglo-Norman institutions of town and castle developed in Ireland, imitating the political and social order of England, and exerting English authority wherever possible. Later, the English influence in Ireland led to the formation of Anglo-Irish society, a class which became associated with the landowners, or the "Big House."

In the writings of early Gaelic poets can be found descriptions of a way of life and a common culture shared by all ranks of Irish through the medium of their native language and the sense of an immemorial past. Some of the old Gaelic houses, especially in Munster, had escaped destruction and English influence. In these districts, the system with the lord's large house and peasant cottages sharing a location, that is, the traditional Big House and Cabin continued as before. Corkery notes how this shared culture affected the social order:

Perhaps the unity that existed between Big House and cabin in the Gaelic districts was a phenomenon not known anywhere else in Europe, inasmuch as feudalism in Ireland had never been quite the same as feudalism abroad.

... It is, then, very probably, correct to say that the divisions of the whole nation into high and low was very different in Ireland from what it was elsewhere; there was surely less of a gap. [20]

This unity must not be underestimated in considering the tenacity of spiritual values of the Irish. Through the windows of early Gaelic poems may be glimpsed a way of life to marvel at. This 18th century poem written in Gaelic, from Corkery's chapter, "The Big House," may portray the atmosphere of an Irish noble house in the seventeenth and eighteenth centuries. [21]

1600s and 1700s Music in Gaelic Big Houses

> *Puirt ar chruitibh dá seinm go ceolmhar,*
> Airs being played harmoniously on harps,
> *Startha dá léigheadh ag lucht léighinn is eolius,*
> The wise and learned reading histories,
> *Mar a mbíodh trácht gan cháim ar órdaibh,*
> In which an account was faultlessly given of the clergy,
> *Is ar gach sloinneadh dar geineadh san Eoruip.*
> And of each great family that arose in Europe.

In a livelier setting, we see the boisterous crowd and the importance of the music, "the sweetness of gentle song in tune:"

> *Ol is imirt, ceol ar fhidil,*
> Drinking, gambling, violins,
> *Beol-ghuth binneas ciuin ceart,*
> The sweetness of gentle song in tune,
> *Fóirne ar mire mór le meisce,*
> A crowd uproariously drunk,
> *Is cóip le sult ag súgradh.*
> And a band eager for merriment.

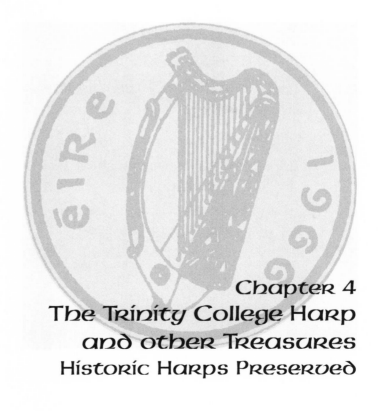

Chapter 4
The Trinity College Harp
and other Treasures
Historic Harps Preserved

Chapter 4~ The Trinity College Harp and other Treasures

Historic Harps Preserved

1014   *Brian Boru defeats the Vikings at Clontarf*
        Legend of the Brian Boru harp begins

Fifteenth Century

1400   *Trinity College Harp originates in Ireland*
        Queen Mary and Lamont Harps originate in Scotland

Sixteenth Century

1521   *"Brian Boru" harp sent from Pope to King Henry VIII*

1534   *Engravings of harps on the Irish coins of Henry VIII*

Seventeenth & Eighteenth Centuries

1621   *Dalway-Fitzgerald (Cloyne) harp is made in Ireland*

1760   *Harper Arthur O'Neil plays ancient harp in Limerick*

1782   *Harp played by O'Neil presented to Trinity College*

Nineteenth & Twentieth Centuries

1840   *Edward Bunting publishes detailed study*
        of Trinity College Harp

1904   *R.B. Armstrong's complete study,*
        The Irish and the Highland Harps

A famous medieval Irish harp, affectionately known as the "Brian Boru Harp," is on display at the Library of Trinity College, Dublin, near the equally famous Book of Kells. This harp is remarkable as one of the finest examples of a medieval musical instrument. As a symbol of their heritage, it has continued to inspire succeeding generations of Irish men and women, at home and abroad, with evidence of the ancient culture of Ireland.

The Trinity College Harp belongs with two other 15th century harps that have survived intact over time: the Queen Mary Harp and the Lamont Harp, both from the 15th century in Scotland. Along with one other preserved harp, the Dalway-Fitzgerald Harp from 17th century Ireland, these instruments tell much about the station of the harp in earlier centuries. These four historic harps originally were strung with wire strings and played with long pointed fingernails, used like plectra. The harp would rest on the left shoulder, with the left hand playing in the treble, the right hand in the bass.

An image of the Trinity College Harp appears today on every Irish coin, even as it first occurred on coins in the time of King Henry VIII of England. The custom of presenting an image of some type of harp on the coins of Ireland predates Henry's time and has been modified over the years. Since 1926, each of the new Irish coins has carried a beautiful new image of the Trinity College harp.

THE HARP OF BRIAN BORU, HIGH KING OF IRELAND

The Trinity College Harp is associated by legend with the first High King of Ireland, Brian Boru, who is said to have played the harp himself, or at least had his personal harper with him during his exploits. Brian Boru, patron of the arts and learning as well as a warrior, was king of Munster for 37 years, from A.D. 965 to 1002. With his leadership, Ireland was united for the first time under a single king in the years 1002 to 1014. Brian's last battle is well known to the Irish — how he fought the Viking invaders at the Battle of Clontarf in A.D. 1014. It was an historic battle in which the Norsemen, who had plundered Irish lands for over two centuries, were routed. Sadly, as he knelt in prayer in his hour of victory, the 73 year-old King Brian was slaughtered by the enemy. [22]

1014
Brian Boru
defeats the
Vikings

According to this legend, after the death of Brian his son Donogh, who eventually became king, took possession of Brian's harp. Much later while on a state visit to Rome in 1062, Donogh bequeathed his father's harp to the Pope. This harp is said to have remained as one of the treasures of the Vatican for almost four hundred years until 1521 when Pope Leo X sent the harp to King Henry VIII in England. The occasion for such a gift was the Pope's proclamation of King Henry as "Defender of the Faith," an ironic title for this king. Some twenty years later in Ireland, the native Catholics would be overthrown as this same Henry turned against his faith and against the Irish as the new Protestant king of Ireland.

1521
Brian Boru
harp to
Henry VIII

Legend also associates the harp of Brian Boru with a harp owned by the O'Brien family of Ireland, a much-prized treasure that is said to have been sent from Ireland to Scotland and back again. [23] Whatever the case may be, this famous harp will always be Brian's harp to many, and even in the scholarly world it is sometimes still called the Brian Boru harp. [24]

HISTORY OF AN ANCIENT HARP

A harp of great antiquity was known to have been played in 1760 by Arthur O'Neill, a prominent Irish harper, in the city of Limerick. In O'Neill's extensive memoirs, recounted to Ed-

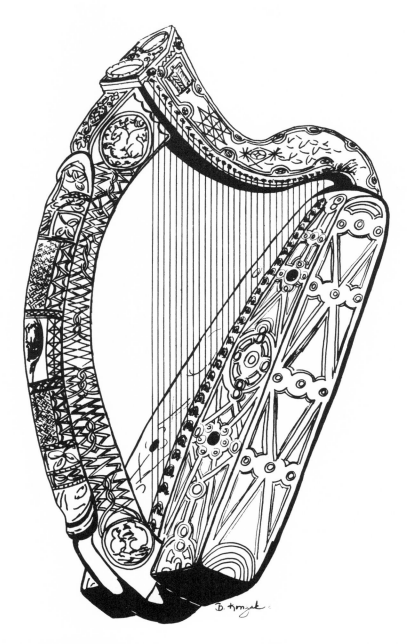

FIGURE 9. THE TRINITY COLLEGE HARP, FROM 15TH CENTURY IRELAND. THIS SKETCH IS BASED ON AN ENGRAVING IN BUNTING'S *A COLLECTION OF THE ANCENT MUSIC OF IRELAND*. IT HAS BEEN ENHANCED TO SHOW THE HARP STRUNG WITH WIRE STRINGS. THIS 30-STRING HARP IS SMALL: ABOUT 33 INCHES TALL AND 18 INCHES WIDE.

> ## ARTHUR O'NEILL'S ACCOUNT OF BRIAN'S HARP
>
> "When I left the County Kerry my next tour was towards Limerick … I met a Counsellor Macnamara, then Recorder of Limerick, … He had a house in Limerick in which was the skeleton of Brian Boru's harp, and in consequence of the national esteem I held for its owner I new strung it and then tuned it. It was made of cedar. It was not strung for upwards of two hundred years before — which when done Counsellor Macnamara requested me to strap it around my neck and play it through that hospitable city, which I agreed to do, being then young and hearty and had no care… and the first tune I happened to strike on was the tune of 'Eileen Óg', now generally called 'Savourneen Deelish' and 'Erin Go Bragh'.
>
> "I played several tunes besides and I was followed by a procession of upwards of five hundred people, both gentle and simple, as they seemed to be every one imbibed with a national spirit when they heard it was the instrument that our celebrated Irish monarch played upon before he leathered the Danes at Clontarf out of poor Erin.
>
> "The Lord be merciful to you, Brian Boru! I hope in God I will tune your harp again in your presence in heaven. And if it should be the case, upon my honour and conscience I will not play the tunes of 'July the First' nor 'The Protestant Boys'; but I would willingly play 'God Save the King', and that would be for yourself, Brian!"
>
> *Words of harper Arthur O'Neill, as dictated in 1810 to Edward Bunting.* [25]

ward Bunting in 1810, one passage tells how O'Neill came upon an ancient harp, restrung it, and wandered the streets of Limerick singing praise for Ireland and honor for King Brian (see above text from O'Neill).

Eventually this harp was presented to Trinity College in 1782 and is still preserved there. Whether this particular harp belonged to King Brian Boru or made distant journeys is debatable. Storytellers would like to link this splendid instrument with the valorous king who united Ireland and drove out her enemies, but facts seem otherwise. Dr. George Petrie, an eminent Irish historian in the late 19th century, examined the Trinity College Harp and studied its history, concluding that the harp originated early in the 15th century. Its similarity to the Queen Mary Harp of Scotland suggests to some that it may have been crafted in the West Highlands of Scotland. [26]

1782 Harp given to Trinity College

Edward Bunting made a careful study of the Trinity College Harp and published this description in *A Collection of the Ancient Music of Ireland (1840):*

> From recent examination it appears that this harp had but one row of strings; that these were thirty in number …thirty being the number of brass tuning pins and of corresponding string holes. It is thirty-two inches high, and of exquisite workmanship; the upright pillar is of oak, and the soundboard of red sallow; the extremity of the forearm or harmonic curved bar is capped in part with silver, extremely well wrought and chiseled. It also contains a large crystal set in silver, under which was another stone, now lost." [27]

1840 Bunting's study of Trinity College Harp

Bunting goes on to describe the expert workmanship of the silver ornamentation and the "minute and beautiful carving which on all parts of this instrument attests the high state of the ornamental arts in Ireland at this period." Bunting includes fine engravings of the harp in his books, and in these drawings the harp is pictured without strings.

In addition to Bunting's work, a detailed study of the Trinity College Harp and other historic harps was published by Robert Bruce Armstrong in 1904 in Edinburgh. This extraordinary book, *The Irish and the Highland Harps*, is illustrated generously with meticulous drawings made by the author as well as with photographs. Armstrong demonstrated that this harp had been damaged and then improperly repaired at some time between Bunting's time and his, and that it was then distorted several inches out of shape by the crude addition of an extension at the base of the harp.

TRINITY COLLEGE HARP RESTORED IN 1961

In 1961, a professional restoration of the famous harp was done at the British Museum in London. At this time the instrument was carefully photographed, x-rayed for the location of metal parts, measured and examined, and then skillfully dismantled. Using modern techniques the harp was carefully repaired and restored to its original form and the decorative work was renewed.

The ancient harp was then restrung with fine brass wire, and allowed to be played by several Irish harpists. It proved to have an unusual, clear, bell-like tone. The sound of the Trinity College Harp was recorded by the BBC at the time, then the strings were slackened off lest the harp be damaged again by the strain. This demonstration started a revival of interest in the sound of the wire-strung harps of medieval Ireland. [28]

THE QUEEN MARY AND LAMONT HARPS
FROM 15TH CENTURY SCOTLAND

Two other excellent examples of medieval harps can be seen at the National Museum of Antiquities of Scotland, in Edinburgh. These 15th century Scottish harps, very similar to the Trinity College Harp, are a reminder of the close cultural ties between Scotland and Ireland. These impressive Scottish harps are dealt with extensively by Armstrong in the "Highland Harp" section of his book, *The Irish and the Highland Harps*. A more recent discussion of the harps of Scotland and Ireland appears in *The Tree of Strings*, a complete study by Keith Sanger and Allison Kinnard.

c. 1400 Queen Mary Harp, Scotland

The Queen Mary Harp is a work of art, beautifully wrought. The forepillar is principally shaped in the form of a double-headed reptile, while the soundbox terminates at the base in the form of a dog's head. A few inches shorter than the Trinity College Harp, the Queen Mary Harp has twenty-nine holes for strings in its soundbox. The entire harp is decorated with relief carvings and pokerwork in intricate Celtic patterns of vines, interlaced with stylized animal and reptile forms.

c. 1400 Lamont Harp, Scotland

The Lamont Harp is of similar form but larger than the others. This harp, which is pictured lying on its back in Armstrong's book, is just over three feet high, still a small harp

FIGURE 10: QUEEN MARY HARP, 15TH CENTURY SCOTLAND. ABOUT 30 INCHES TALL, 18 INCHES WIDE. THIS SKETCH, BASED ON A DRAWING FROM BUNTING'S WORK, SHOWS THE HARP FULLY STRUNG.[11]

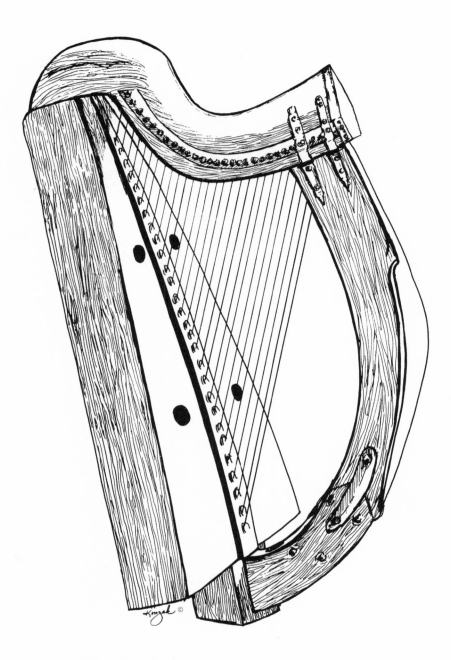

FIGURE 11. LAMONT HARP, 15ᵀᴴ CENTURY SCOTLAND. THIRTY-TWO STRING HOLES IN THE SOUNDBOX, 37 INCHES TALL, AND 20 INCHES WIDE. DRAWING SHOWS THE HARP IN A RESTRUNG CONDITION.

by any measure. Medieval harps were usually placed on their backs while not being played; the image of the upright historical harp is a modern illusion. With the same one-piece soundbox and sturdy construction, the Lamont Harp is a beautiful instrument, although it is not so elegantly carved and decorated as the Trinity College or the Queen Mary Harps.

The Dalway, or Cloyne harp from 17th Century Ireland

1621 Dalway-Fitzgerald / Cloyne harp

An elegant harp made in 1621 is used as the frontispiece of Edward Bunting's second collection, *The Ancient Music of Ireland*, published in 1809. This harp was originally made for Sir John Fitzgerald of Cloyne, and has been known both by the name of its first owner and that of a later owner, Noah Dalway. Only fragments of the original harp still exist today: the carved pillar and the arm, or harmonic curve, are at the National Museum of Ireland in Dublin.

Like the Trinity College Harp of the 15th century, this beautiful instrument has been damaged and restored several times. *The Irish and the Highland Harps* describes the Dalway harp in minute detail with drawings and photographs, as well as covering Robert Bruce Armstrong's own contribution to its restoration at that time around the turn of the century. A re-

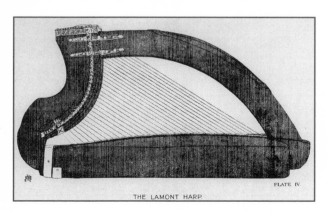

Figure 12. The Lamont Harp as drawn by R.B. Armstrong, in *The Irish and The Highland Harps*.

THE LAMONT HARP

PLATE IV.

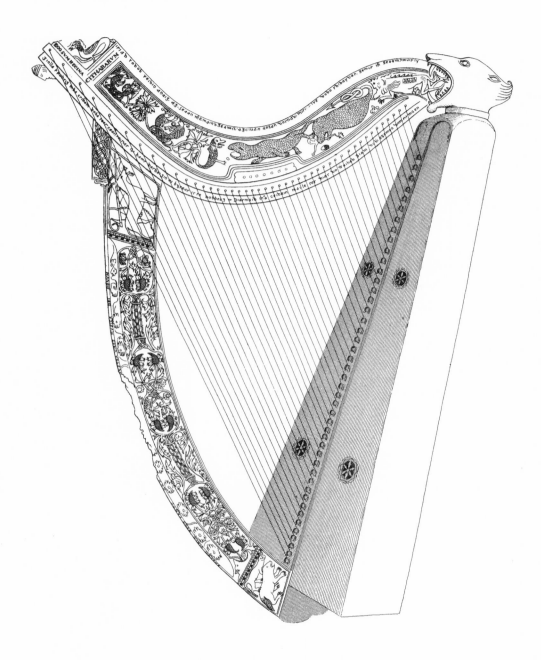

FIGURE 13. DALWAY HARP, 17TH CENTURY IRELAND. ABOUT 25 INCHES
TALL, WITH 45 PIN-HOLES IN THE NECK, AND SEVEN ADDITIONAL HOLES.

cent restoration, or replication of this harp was completed in 1996, commissioned by the National Museum of Ireland. Harpmaker Robert Evans brought together original materials and techniques to create an exact copy of the harp, now called the "Cloyne harp" to identify its place of origin.

Of the remaining fragments, the harmonic curve is about 35 inches long, the pillar about 33 inches. The original harp had a full row of 45 pinholes in the neck plus seven additional holes above the main row, centered in mid-scale. In Bunting's illustration, the secondary row of strings is not shown, but fully strung the harp would have had 52 strings, suggesting that it was tuned as a chromatic harp with strings for both sharps and flats. [28]

The Dalway or Cloyne harp is remarkable for its marvelous ornamentation. Every inch of the existing fragments is decorated in artistic detail with Celtic imagery. A fantasy of animals, reptiles, and little creatures playing musical instruments issues from the mouth of a dog's head, which surmounts the sounding board and provides the connecting shoulder of the harp. The pillar is elaborately carved with Celtic interlacing patterns of leaves, flowers, and fruit.

The date, 1621, and the coat-of-arms of the Fitzgerald family adorn the front of the pillar, which is headed with a carved figure of a queen. Inscribed above the figures is *Ego Sum Regina Citharum*, Latin for "I am the Queen of Harps." Other inscriptions in both Latin and Irish note the history of the harp, its owner, maker, and harpers who have played it.

The decorative work on this historic harp is similar to the fascinating Celtic ornamentation of the 8th century *Book of Kells*. The fine detail work is lightened by the inclusion of whimsical creatures and persons. This playful touch, in the presence of solemnity, is a notable trait of the Irish, who are generally on good terms with fairies and all the little people.

The Carved Out Soundbox

It is the soundbox fashioned out of a single trunk of a willow tree that made the ancient wire-strung harps the object of so much attention and respect in medieval Europe. Robert Bruce Armstrong provides descriptions and illustrations of this in *The Irish and The Highland Harps*: "The box or trunk of the Ancient Harp was usually in the form of a truncated triangle, and was invariably constructed out of a solid piece of timber, which was hollowed out from the back so as to form the sides, ends, and sounding-board, the cavity being covered at the back by a board." [29]

Armstrong goes on to discuss the durability of this type of construction: "The duration of time which the Celtic Harp....remained a serviceable instrument was limited by the power of the sounding-board to resist the tension of the strings. The harmonic curve and fore-pillar could be replaced if damaged.... [but] the purity and sweetness of tone was mainly due to the construction of the box, which, musically speaking, was the most important part of the instrument." [30]

On why the ancient Irish and Scottish harpmakers always used this method, Armstrong notes that glue or another method of building up a sound box for the harp could have been used; it was not for lack of woodworking ability that this method was chosen. The reason of course is clear — a carved out soundbox was used to build harps because of the unusual strength it gave to the instrument, which in turn provided its beautiful tone.

Armstrong's opinion was echoed by current day harper Derek Bell, in his memory of something Roland Robinson, founder of the Folk Harp Journal, once told him: "Mr. R.L. Robinson, the distinguished California harp maker, once suggested to me that it was his considered opinion that the Irish harp was by far the most strongly constructed instrument in

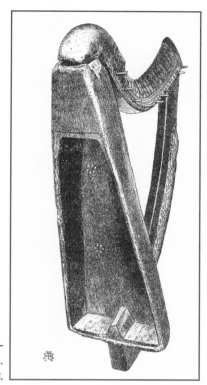

FIGURE 14. BACK OF THE CASTLE OTWAY HARP, PIC-
TURED WITHOUT ITS COVERING BOARD, AS DRAWN BY R.
B. ARMSTRONG, *THE IRISH AND THE HIGHLAND HARPS*.

the Renaissance period. … its tone was far superior to that of
any keyboard instrument of the times."[31]

The strength of this construction method and the crafts-
manship with which these beautiful harps were made is being
replicated widely by craftspeople today.

We turn next to some of the difficult history of Ireland, to
help in understanding the decline of the bardic traditions, and
the making and playing of these treasured instruments.

Engraved by John Kirkwood Dublin

Ancient Irish Harp in Trinity College Dublin
Left Hand Side View

FIGURE 15. TRINITY COLLEGE HARP. ENGRAVING BY JOHN KIRKWOOD, DUBLIN, FROM THE ANCIENT MUSIC OF IRELAND BY EDWARD BUNTING.

Chapter 5
Suppression of the Irish
Historical Background,
the 12th to 17th Centuries

Chaper 5 ~ Suppression of the Irish Historical Background, the 14th to 17th Centuries

Twelfth to Fourteenth Centuries

c. 1200 Anglo-Norman invasion of Ireland

1366   Statute of Kilkenny, an attempt to ban English-Irish assimilation

Sixteenth Century

1535   Henry VIII declares himself Head of the Church of England

1541   Henry VIII becomes King of Ireland

1558   Elizabeth I begins her reign

1576   Privy Council laws banish Irish harpers

Seventeenth Century

1607   Flight of the Earls, exile to the Continent

1608   Plantation of Ulster, Irish lands given to settlers

1646   Owen Roe O'Neill, the Liberator, leads a revolt

1649   Oliver Cromwell crushes Catholic Ireland

1690   Flight of the Wild Geese

By the end of the twelfth century, the Anglo-Norman invasions and gradual conquest of Ireland brought foreign dominion and large changes in the fortunes of the native Irish. Previous to 1156 when King Henry II of England got authority from the Pope to take possession of the island, the Irish were ruled by powerful chieftains who were important heads of clans. However, when the Anglo-Normans arrived in Leinster in 1170 with two hundred knights and a thousand men-at-arms, the Irish were easily overtaken. In *A History of Modern Ireland*, Giovanni Costigan explains what happened to the ancient, unwritten Gaelic set of customs that had successfully governed Irish lands for centuries:

> By 1260… the Brehon laws based upon communal property in land were swept away, and feudal ownership was established in their place. This change involved a sudden, violent breach of customs that were well over a thousand years old. The Irish were either driven from the river valleys into the bogs and forests or else were suffered to remain as serfs – to till the lands of their conquerors. [32]

c. 1200 Anglo-Norman invasion of Ireland

The Anglo-Normans, as a people, were the product of an earlier invasion of what is now England by the Normans from France. At that time, mid-eleventh century, the two cultures (Anglos and Normans) became easily assimilated, later coming to be known simply as the English. However, when the Anglo-Normans invaded Ireland and encountered the native Irish, it was an entirely different story. Costigan continues: "... the two peoples remained tragically divided, each hating and despising the other. Throughout the Middle Ages in Ireland, there were really two nations, not one: Anglo-Norman Ireland, based on town and castle, with its earls, barons, and knights; and the old Gaelic Ireland whose social order was still rooted in the tribal customs of the Celts." [33]

Despite the animosity between the two peoples, there was much intermarrying between the Anglo-Norman settlers and the native Irish, and in the process Irish customs gradually became adopted by the invaders.

In a vain attempt to prevent the assimilation of the Anglo-Normans into the native Irish culture, England enacted the Statute of Kilkenny in 1366, making marriage between English and Irish a capital crime. Englishmen living in Ireland (the Anglo-Normans) were also prohibited from speaking the Irish language, singing Irish airs, and playing Irish music — particularly the harp. An Englishman could not wear the kilt or adopt any other Irish customs. In addition, receiving or entertaining Irish harpers, rhymers, or others considered seditious by the British Crown was made a penal offense. This 14th-century attempt to eliminate a culture was impossible to enforce and a process of assimilation continued.

1366 Statute of Kilkenny bans Irish - English marriage

Usurpation of Ireland by Henry VIII

After Martin Luther's defiance of the Pope in 1517, the spirit of the Reformation began to agitate Western Europe in the 16th century, but Catholic Ireland remained loyal to the Pope. This religious position by the Irish, in addition to the political situation, became an excuse for the exercise of abusive power by English monarchs.

When Henry VIII came to the throne of England as a young man of nineteen in 1509, the power of the Crown in Ireland

Figure 16: "Henry VIII Harp Groat - H & A.", Irish coin, circa 1534. Inscription translated: Henry VIII by the Grace of God King of England and France and Lord of Ireland.

1524
Early laws
against
Irish bards
was nominal. However, as time went on, new attempts were made to prevent the spread of Irish culture and to oppress the Irish people. Henry's arrogance in regard to the Irish included his use of the ancient Irish harp on coins proclaiming himself King of England and Lord of Ireland (figure 16.)

In the year 1524, upon pain of fine or imprisonment, the first enactment against Irish bards and minstrels during Henry's time was made. In the language of the time, it read, in part: "That noe Irish minstralls rymers, ne bardes, be messengers to desire any goods of any man dwelling within the English Pale." This order was pronounced but seldom heeded by the nobles of the English Pale who, following the example of Irish lords such as the Earls of Kildare, Desmond, and Ormonde, often retained their own Irish harper. [34]

1527
Henry
initiates
Protestant
refomation
in England
By 1527, anxious for a male heir and wanting to be rid of his current queen, Henry applied to the Pope for permission to divorce and was refused. Repudiating the Pope, Henry had his first marriage declared null and proceeded with his second marriage. When, in 1535, by virtue of the Act of Supremacy passed by the English Parliament, Henry declared himself to be "Supreme Head of the Church of England," the repercussions in Ireland were immediate. For Henry the object was divorce, but the issue was the authority of the King of England versus the Pope, with the future of Ireland hanging in the balance.

Under the guise of granting titles of nobility to native Irish chieftains, a land reform policy begun by Henry VIII destroyed the existing Irish system of hereditary land tenure. In its place, the English feudal system with its laws of primogeniture, proclaimed all land to be derived from the Crown and that the eldest son should inherit all property and titles. This usurpation by the English monarch of both the spiritual and the worldly rights of the Irish led to war.

"Silken Thomas" FitzGerald, inspired by Harper's Song

The most powerful family in 15th century Ireland was the lineage of the Earls of Kildare, who were of Anglo-Norman origns. Under the policies of Henry VIII, the Ninth Earl of Kildare was held several times on charges of treason against the Crown; in 1534 this earl was held in the Tower of London where he died in captivity. His son, Thomas FitzGerald, Tenth Earl of Kildare, led a brave but unsucessful revolt. Thomas, a friend of rhymers and harpers, identified with the fortunes of the native Irish and was known as "Silken Thomas" (his men wore silk tassels on their helmets). The following account written in 1905 by the historian W. H. Flood is a tale that must have been well known at that time:

> All readers of Irish history are familiar with the dramatic incident which happened on June 11th, 1534, when O'Keenan, … harper to Silken Thomas, struck up an Irish song in praise of his lord, at St. Mary's Abbey, Dublin, with the result that the impetuous Geraldine [FitzGerald] threw down his sword of state and went into rebellion. [35]

For nearly a year Silken Thomas and his seven thousand men controlled much of Leinster from his stronghold, the Castle at Maynooth. In another tale of the famous hero, Thomas is a musician, playing his harp beneath the branches of a famous yew tree just before his downfall. The English army, two-thousand strong and with siege artillery, overran the castle, crushing the revolt. Silken Thomas and his party were held and ceremoniously beheaded in London in 1537. [36] That same year, the English Parliament declared Henry VIII "Supreme Head of the Church in Ireland."

Shortly after the revolt of Silken Thomas, the suppression of Irish monasteries and confiscation of property began. In 1541, Henry VIII, not satisfied with being both the king of England and head of the church, had himself declared King of Ireland as well. Henceforth a new unity against a common enemy, the English Crown, would develop between the na-

1534 Rebellion of Silken Thomas

1541 Henry VIII declared King of Ireland

tive Irish and the gradually-assimilated descendents of the Anglo-Normans. This new group came to be known as the Anglo-Irish — the class associated with landowners and those who could afford to support the art of the wandering harpers.

The Elizabethan Age and Irish Music

*1558
Rein of
Elizabeth I
(Elizabethan
Age) begins*

With the ascent to the throne of England in 1558 by Elizabeth I , daughter of Henry VIII, the schism involving church-related loyalties worsened. The native Irish and the Anglo-Irish remained Catholic, while English interests were identified as Protestant. Despite the rebellions and unrest in Ireland, Irish music flourished in the court of Queen Elizabeth and the elegant music period known as the Renaissance flowered.

Irish music was enjoyed widely throughout England. The queen herself retained an Irish harper in her retinue, and the dancing of native Irish jigs by Anglo-Irish ladies of the Court was much admired. Harp playing continued to be favored and many of the noble houses of both the Irish and Anglo-Irish maintained their own harpers, in spite of strictures against certain classes of musicians. Increasingly, however, Irish harpers came into disfavor with the Queen because of their loyalty to their Irish lords.

*1563
First
Elizabethan
laws against
"Rhymers &
Bardes"*

The first Elizabethan enactment against "Rymours, Bardes, dice-players," and other such miscreants was legislated in 1563. The stated reason was that "under pretense of visiting, they [musicians] carry about privy intelligence between the malefactors in the disturbed districts." [37] There was some truth to this fear of underground activity; the Irish harpers and bards had little allegiance to their English lords.

During the 1570s, "various commissions were issued by Queen Elizabeth I in Ireland to 'banish all Irish harpers,' and, in 1576, the Privy Council in London issued stringent orders

FIGURE 17. SOME HISTORICAL SITES IN IRELAND, ALONG WITH MODERN BOUNDARIES.

1576
Privy
Council
banishes
Irish
harpers

against 'rhymers, harpers, and other Irishmen' within the English Pale.'" [38] That the period of Queen Elizabeth was an illustrious one for England is well known. It was a time of conquest of men and nature. It was also the beginning of the end of the old Gaelic order in Ireland.

ANNEXATION, REVOLT, AND DEFEAT

The first wholesale annexation of Irish land by England, the Plantation of Munster, was done in the name of Queen Elizabeth I. An uprising led by the Desmond family of Munster in 1579 led to retaliation in the form of a brutal massacre partly carried out under the command of Sir Walter Raleigh. By 1584, half a million acres of Irish land had been confiscated for the Crown. Devastation was wrought in Munster, historically known as a center of Gaelic learning and bardic schools. Great forests were cut, civilians slaughtered, the land laid waste, and the surviving population scattered.

1584
Plantation
of Munster

HUGH O'NEILL AND RED HUGH O'DONNELL

Toward the end of the 16th century the Irish were heartened by a series of victories against the British under the leadership of Hugh O'Neill, Earl of Tyrone, and his son-in-law, Red Hugh O'Donnell. For a time it seemed as if they would be successful in throwing off the English, but the Irish forces were defeated on Christmas Eve, 1601, in the decisive battle of Kinsale. Donal O'Sullivan, biographer of Turlough O'Carolan, comments on this turning point: "The battle of Kinsale marked the end of Irish independence in any form for three centuries, and also the end of that system wherein learned poets and harpers had found a natural place." [39]

1601
Irish defeat
at Battle
of Kinsale

THE FLIGHT OF THE EARLS AND PLANTATION OF ULSTER

A sorry postscript to Kinsale was the "Flight of the Earls" in September 1607, in which the heads of the two great tribes of Ulster went sadly into exile. Fearing arrest, Hugh O'Neill, Earl of Tyronne, persuaded Rory O'Donnell, the younger brother of Red Hugh and by then Earl of Tyrconnell, to accompany him in leaving Ireland for the Continent. With one hundred followers, mainly nobles of Ulster, the earls traveled through France and finally were received by the Pope in Rome, where they took residence and were later buried. The flight of these Irish lords dramatically symbolized the collapse of the old Irish society and the defeat of the Gaels.

1607
Flight of
the Earls

With the noblemen gone, the conquerors proceeded to confiscate their lands, taking over a large portion of the north of Ireland. The Plantation of Ulster, six counties comprising two million acres, were handed over to Protestant settlers from England and Scotland. The Irish landowners who had not already left were driven out or reduced to servitude.

1608
Plantation
of Ulster

THE SPIRIT OF IRELAND, DARK ROSALEEN

About this time there arose a poem of pathetic hope, "Dark Rosaleen," which evoked the spirit of Ireland as that of a young, beautiful, grieving woman. It was originally written in the Gaelic by Costello of Ballyhaunis, a bard attached to the O'Donnell family. Two hundred years later another Irishman, James Clarance Mangan, transformed the song into English verse:

> O my Dark Rosaleen!
>   Do not sigh, do not weep!
> The priests are on the ocean green,
>   They march along the deep.
>
> There's wine from the royal Pope
>   Upon the ocean green,

FIGURE 18. IMAGE OF IRELAND, SIR JOHN LAVERY'S PAINTING OF HIS WIFE, FIRST USED ON THE CURRENCY OF THE IRISH FREE STATE IN 1923, AND CONTINUED ON PAPER MONEY UNTIL THE 1970S.

> And Spanish ale shall give you hope,
>> My dark Rosaleen!
>> My own Rosaleen!
> Shall glad your heart, shall give you hope,
> Shall give you health, and help, and hope,
>> My dark Rosaleen! [40]

Much later still, in the early 1920s, Sir John Lavery painted another image of this spirit of Ireland, the lady who appeared posing with her harp on Irish bank notes for many years.

IRELAND RISES TO BE CRUSHED AGAIN

It was not until 1641 that the demoralized Irish were able to rise in rebellion; an insurrection in the North against English settlers that resulted in a number of Protestants being killed. This date would long be remembered in Ulster.

1646 Owen Roe O'Neill leads an Irish revolt

The old Irish stock rallied under Owen Roe O'Neill, a nephew of Hugh O'Neill, called out of exile after having served in the armies of Spain for thirty years. Owen O'Neill won a notable victory in 1646 at Benburb, County Tyrone, and was hailed as "the Liberator" by the jubilant Irish. His mysterious death three years later, however, put an end to their hopes. Owen Roe O'Neill was to be eulogized by the famous 17th-century harper, Turlough O' Carolan in his song titled simply "Owen O'Neill." Looked to in modern times as an Irish hero, Owen Roe O'Neill was one of the first leaders with a vision of a United Ireland.

OLIVER CROMWELL AND THE CROMWELLIAN SETTLEMENT

Oliver Cromwell, the tyrannical English Puritan, was sent to Ireland in 1649 to rout the Catholics, which he did with such savage vengeance that soon all resistance was broken. The people were decimated by war, disease, and starvation. Under terms of the Cromwellian Settlement, all estates east of the Shannon River were forfeited, and the surviving populations of Ireland's most fertile provinces were uprooted and forced to move to the poor territory of Connacht in the west.

The Cromwellian Settlement was even more disastrous for Catholic Ireland than the Plantation of Ulster had been, for it meant the appropriation of almost eight million acres of Irish soil, almost half of the cultivable land in the island, and redistribution of ancestral lands to Protestant settlers. Henceforth, the name Drogheda, site of the Cromwellian siege and massacre of 1649, would be intoned lamentably. [41]

THE FLIGHT OF THE WILD GEESE

The defeat of Catholic forces at the decisive Battle of the Boyne, by the army of William of Orange, was followed one year later by an overwhelming defeat at Aughrim, County Galway. Soon after, Limerick was lost in spite of the heroic defense led by Patrick Sarsfield, later to become an important national hero of modern Ireland. These events precipitated the exodus deplored as the flight of the "Wild Geese," when Sarsfield and thousands of his fighting men went into exile in France, ending the hopes of 17th century Catholic Ireland.

END OF THE OLD BARDIC ORDER IN IRELAND

Such upheavals spelled the end of the old bardic order as it had been known in Ireland since before Christ, though aspects of the tradition persisted in out of the way places. Families that had for centuries been patrons of the poets and harpers had been ousted by English incursions, their lands and entire estates confiscated. The planters who succeeded them were a new landlord class of Cromwellian officers and English speculators, not supporters of traditional Gaelic arts. Harp playing, once an esteemed profession, became a more modest occupation.

1695
Start of the
Penal Laws

The style of the Irish arts changed, too, as poetry of the high, old style gave way to popular verse and melodic tunes. At the height of medieval minstrelsy, three expert artists would create the atmosphere: the poet as composer of verse, the *reacaire* or speaker, and the harper playing the music. By the 17th century, these three skills were often merged into one performer.

Toward the end of the 17th century, there were a few native families who had not been dispossessed, and who began to cultivate both native Irish and European music. To these families, we owe the patronage of Turlough O'Carolan, the famous harper who lived during the desperate period of the Penal Laws in Ireland

Begun in 1695, these laws systematically deprived Catholics of all civil, religious, educational, and property rights, resulting in an almost total destruction of the old social order in Ireland. There were huge clearances of fields and forests as new lords took over lands that had been held in common by the people, and many head of Irish cattle were set upon the roads to Irish ports to be shipped to England. As Daniel Corkery writes in *The Hidden Ireland*, "the result of all was that herds of dispossessed human beings, as well as the herds of beasts, began to darken the roads."[42]

Turlough O'Carolan, however, traveling along these same roads, remained unprejudiced and pursued his calling and the traditions of his profession as best he could in the adversity of the times, being equally welcome in the homes of both Catholics and Protestants alike.

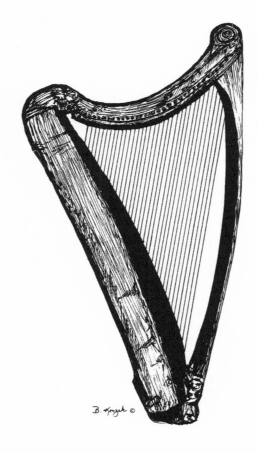

carolan's harp

FIGURE 19. LARGE HIGH-HEADED HARP OF TURLOUGH O'CAROLAN. PILLAR, NECK AND ONE-PIECE SOUNDBOX ARE SYCAMORE; HARP HAS 35 STRING HOLES.[4] DRAWING SHOWS HARP AS IT MAY HAVE LOOKED WHEN FULLY STRUNG.

Chapter 6
Turlough O'Carolan
Irish Harper-Composer, 1670 - 1738

Chapter 6~ Turlough O'Carolan
Irish Harper-Composer, 1670 - 1738

Late Seventeenth Century

1670 Turlough O'Carolan born in County Meath

1684 Turlough, age 14, moves with family
to Roscommon area

1688 Carolan becomes blind at age 18
begins training as harper, helped by Mrs. MacDermott

1693 Turlough O'Carolan marries Mary Maguire,
settles on farm, begins travels and composing

1695 Penal Laws enacted, depriving Irish of civil rights

Early Eighteenth Century

1730s "Carolan's Concerto" composed

1738 Turlough O'Carolan's "Farewell to Music"

1738 March 25, Death of Turlough O'Carolan

Born in the latter part of the 17th century, Turlough O'Carolan is famous both as a harper and as a composer. He is known and loved for his gift of melody and his rendering of music on the harp for the pleasure of his countrymen. Carolan (as he is known) composed by ear and committed to memory over two hundred songs, chiefly in honor of his patrons. He played and sang to his own harp accompaniment in the many homes, both Irish and Anglo-Irish, that he visited in the course of his travels in Ireland. A large, high-headed harp (figure 19, page 74), said to have belonged to Carolan, is preserved in the National Museum of Ireland in Dublin.

*1670
Birth of
Turlough
O'Carolan*

Turlough O'Carolan led his early life near Nobber, County Meath, where he was born in 1670, the son of John Carolan, a native Irish blacksmith and farmer. When Turlough was about fourteen, his family moved to the Roscommon-Leitrim district where his father found employment at the Iron foundry, operated by the MacDermott Roe family at Ballyfarnon. The lady of the house, Mrs. MacDermott Roe, took an interest in the boy and assisted with his education. Young Turlough learned to read Irish well and some English, however, at the age of eighteen he lost his sight due to smallpox and became totally blind. Mrs. MacDermott Roe then placed him in the training of a practicing harper and supported him for three years while he became an accomplished musician. Mrs. MacDermott provided him with a horse and a guide, and at the age of twenty-one Turlough O' Carolan began his long career as a traveling harper.

*1688
Carolan
becomes
blind, trains
as a harper*

Carolan's first sweetheart, before he lost his sight, was Bridget Cruise of County Meath and several tender airs were composed for her. At the age of twenty-three, he married Mary

Maguire of County Fermanagh and settled with her on a small farm in County Leitrim, where they had four daughters and a son. Carolan's career took him away from home for long periods of time for he regularly traveled to the west central parts of Ireland, in the province of Connacht, making occasional longer trips, including to Dublin.

1693
Carolan
marries,
travels the
countryside

A LINK TO THE GAELIC PAST

While on the road, Carolan would compose the piece to be played at his next house of call, keeping both melody and verse in memory. The tunes came first, then Carolan would add words to honor his host that would be sung or recited while playing the harp. Donal O'Sullivan, in his biography of Carolan, describes the scene:

> … two men on horseback, one a blind harper, the other his guide carrying his harp, plodding along the bad roads of Ireland in most weathers and at all seasons of the year … eventually reaching a destination where … their coming was often unexpected, but where a welcome awaited them for lovers of music and song, …a certain quiet joy at their arrival. [43]

Carolan's patrons were descendents of the old Gaelic families as well as many English and Scottish newcomers. Remaining Catholic all his life, Carolan was welcomed in all houses, speaking and singing his verse almost exclusively in his native Irish tongue.

A key figure in early 18th century Irish culture, Carolan was a link to what was being lost. "It was through music that many of the Anglo-Irish retained some contact with the Gaelic world," one author points out. "The big-house world that Carolan frequented included many people with a genuine interest in the welfare of the people." [44] The native Irish suffered greatly during these times under restrictions of the Penal Laws. Wandering poets and harpers such as Turlough O'Carolan who passed on Gaelic songs and traditions were especially

FIGURE 20. "CAROLAN'S CONCERTO" AS IT APPEARED IN AN EARLY COLLECTION OF HIS MUSIC.

appreciated by the Irish trying to preserve their love of learning at what were called "hedge schools," small gatherings held out of doors, for lack of access to any other schooling.

COMPOSITIONS BY CAROLAN

Many of Carolan's pieces are named for the subject of his songs, that is, his friends and patrons. These include "Lord Inchiquin," "Miss MacDermott," "John O'Connor," "Bridget Cruise," and "Constantine Maguire." Other pieces such as "Ode to Whiskey," "Carolan's Cottage," and "Carolan's Quarrel with the Landlady" give us a glimpse of the man himself. Much of his music is lively and cheerful, but there are several notable laments, such as the elegy for Owen Roe O'Neill, hero of revolts in the 1640s. Carolan's verses were simple lyrics, sentiments shaped to portray the subject of his song and were subordinate to the melody, for which he is chiefly remembered.

FIGURE 21. BAS-RELIEF OF CAROLAN, PRESENTED BY LADY MORGAN TO ST. PATRICK'S CATHEDRAL IN DUBLIN. SCULPTED BY JOHN VALENTINE HOGAN, IN ROME, C. 1850.

Carolan coined the term "planxty " for a type of lively harp piece, for example: "Planxty Burke," "Planxty O'Rourke," and "Planxty Miss Burke." These pieces were usually in 6/8 meter and did not necessarily have words. Much has been written on the derivation of this term, without conclusive opinion. Possibly, Carolan used the term "planxty" to describe the sound of brisk playing on his wire-strung harp, in the way banjo music is suggested by the words "plinkety-plank."

Carolan greatly admired the music of the Italian composers, Archangelo Corelli and Antonio Vivaldi, his contemporaries, whose works were frequently performed in Dublin early in the 18th century. The piece titled "Carolan's Concerto," totally unlike the melodious songs, is one example of this European influence. The bravura style of this tune could well have given rise to the story that it was composed upon a challenge to display his familiarity with the Italian composers — it is the least Irish of his pieces. Carolan would also have heard the music of J.S. Bach (1685–1750) played in the noble houses of his patrons as he traveled in Ireland.

*1738
Carolan's
Farewell to
Music*

CAROLAN'S FAREWELL TO MUSIC

When Carolan felt that his end was approaching, after nearly fifty years as a traveling harper, he returned to his old home at Alderford, the MacDermott Roe estate. He was warmly welcomed by his aged benefactor, Mrs. MacDermott Roe (nee Mary Fitzgerald). Just before he died, he played for her his last song, "Carolan's Farewell to Music," a rare piece of unusual beauty. In the song, he addressed these words to her in their native Irish tongue:

A Mháire a chroidhe Nic Gearailt,
A run mo chléibh is mo charaid,
Mo léan mar táim Ag sgaruint,
A dhé-bhean d'fhóir dam ions gach céim!

[Mary Fitzgerald, dear heart,
Love of my breast and my friend,
Alas that I am parting from you,
O lady who succored me at every stage!] [45]

When Turlough O'Carolan died in 1738 he was so widely known and loved that his death was an occasion of great shock and grief. His friend Charles O'Conor, wrote in his diary: "Saturday, the 25th day of March, 1738. Turlough O'Carolan, the wise master and chief musician of the whole of Ireland, …died today and was buried in the O'Duigenans' church of Kilronan, in the sixty-eighth year of his age. May his soul find mercy, for he was a moral and religious man." [46]

1721 First collection of Carolan's Music

One hundred twenty years later, about 1858, Lady Louisa Tennison placed an inscription on his grave, with these words: "Within this churchyard lies interred Carolan, the last of the Irish bards." While not strictly a bard in the ancient sense (one who recites the poetry while the harper plays), nor the last harper-composer in the oral tradition, this slogan has long been associated with the memory of Turlough O'Carolan. Certainly he was unique and one of the last of his kind; first and foremost he was a composer of unforgettable melodies.

Music of Carolan Preserved

One small collection of Carolan's music was published in his lifetime, in 1721, when he was on in years. Later, Carolan's son compiled some of his father's music and had it published in Dublin around 1747. This collection, *Music of Carolan,* is one of the earliest surviving examples of printed music in Ireland. Some of Carolan's music was also collected and preserved by his successors. Fifty years after his death, for example, some Carolan tunes were played by harpers and collected by Edward Bunting at the Belfast Harp Festival of 1792.

In addition, many of Carolan's tunes have been passed down via oral tradition to the present day by fiddlers, pipers, and whistle players. The tradition of the Irish *Seisiún,* the playing and teaching of dance tunes, has kept such music alive over the years. In 1971, Derek Bell wrote of Carolan's place as a composer in the preface to a book of music that accompanied Bell's album, *Carolan's Receipt*:

> …True, it [music of Carolan] is composed music and certainly is not entirely folk music, but we owe it to generations of traditional musicians that it has been handed down to us as well as it has been. Indeed, we know, that it has undergone changes and 'improvements' at the hands of countless traditional musicians down through the years. …. The sensible thing to do is simply to regard Carolan's music as part of the tradition even though much of it is not purely traditional style. It is also best to treat it as an Irish traditional musician would, i.e., in an improvisatory style with ornaments and free variations both in good taste and in keeping with the style of each tune. [47]

Although Carolan never wrote down his airs, over two hundred of his melodies exist today, collected and arranged in numerous forms. Turlough O'Carolan is celebrated by all who appreciate Irish traditional music.

Chapter 7
The Irish Harp
Declines, Endures
The 18th and 19th Centuries

Chapter 7~The Irish Harp Declines, Endures

The 18th and 19th Centuries

Early Eighteenth Century

1720   Early pianoforte and single-action pedal harp

Mid-Eighteenth to Early Nineteenth Century

1760   Sebastion Erard, building pianos in France

1789   French Revolution, Erard working in London 1786

1792   Belfast Harp Festival

1796   Edward Bunting's first collection of Irish music

1798   Collapse of Irish rebellion at Wexford

1807   Death of Denis Hempson, master-harper, age 97

1810   Sebastion Erard patents double-action pedal harp

Nineteenth Century

1819   John Egan designs Royal Portable Irish Harp

1840   Publication of Bunting's complete volume,
        "The Ancient Music of Ireland"

Gaelic society, in Ireland, as it had been known for centuries, had nearly collapsed by the end of the 17th century. The Penal Laws of 1695 deprived the Irish of their land, their civil rights, and their way of life. Use of the Irish harp and other traditional arts declined severely. The patterns of society in Ireland changed dramatically, such that many of the old patrons of the harper's art had lost their wealth or were in exile. The poorer, Gaelic-speaking people had intermarried with English and Scottish settlers to form the beginnings of a middle class; this group was not interested in the old style music of the native harpers.

In addition, Romantic styles of music that relied on the use of accidentals had come into vogue; this music was very difficult to play on the traditional Irish harp. Although interest in Irish harp music began to increase at the end of the 18th century, the instrument associated with this once-proud art and the old ways of playing it were dying out.

EMERGENCE OF THE PIANO AND PEDAL HARP

Improvements to the keyboard instruments of previous centuries, resulting in the pianoforte of the 18th century, produced an instrument that would eclipse the harp in widespread usage and general acceptance. Edward Bunting, chronicler of the Irish harp for almost fifty years, took great pains to capture traditional harp music yet he transcribed the music he heard not for the harp, but to be played on the piano. Bunting, like many others of his time, believed that the tradition of playing the Irish harp was a lost art, and that the music would better survive in the piano version.

Progress in the form of an invention, also caused the Irish harp to be put aside in favor of an improved European pedal harp. The piano had become a successful instrument during the 18th century due in part to the work of a Frenchman, Sebastian Erard, who first became prominent as a piano builder in 1760. In 1786, Erard fled from the French Revolution and established a workshop in London, where in 1792 he patented improvements for both the piano and for the pedal harp. Returning to Paris, Erard worked on the design of a pedal mechanism for the harp that would make it possible to change the pitch of a string using foot pedals, freeing the hands. Improving on the work of his many predecessors, in 1810 Erard patented his "double-action" pedal mechanism, making it possible to both raise and lower the pitch of each string without interrupting the playing.

1760
Sebastion Erard builds pianos in France

1810
Erard's double-action pedal harp

By Erard's time, the European harp, which during the Middle Ages had been similar in size to the Irish harp and resembled it in structure, gradually became enlarged. By the mid-eighteenth century this harp was over five feet tall with a straight column, or pillar, to contain rods for the pedals. Erard's invention greatly improved this elaborate instrument, which was eagerly sought by harp players in Great Britain as well as on the Continent and later in America. Professional harpists readily adopted the improved pedal harp as necessary for the complexities of classical music.

THE BELFAST HARP FESTIVAL, 1792

During the latter part of the 18th century, several festivals for the purpose of reviving and perpetuating the ancient music and poetry of Ireland were held in several towns, mostly in Northern Ireland. The most notable of these festivals was the one held in Belfast in July, 1792, in the Assembly Room of the Belfast Exchange. Circulars were sent out the previous year to

1792
Belfast Harp Festival

BUNTING'S DESCRIPTION OF THE BELFAST FESTIVAL

The following text is excerpted from page 63 of Edward Bunting's "The Ancient Music of Ireland," 1840 edition. Reprinted by permission of Waltons Musical Instruments Galleries Inc. Bunting refers to himself here as "the Editor".

Ten harpers only responded to this call, a sufficient proof of the declining state of the art, and of the necessity which now manifestly existed of noting down as many as possible of these musical treasures which might so soon perish along with their venerable repositories. This was the office assigned to the Editor, and in discharging it, he first imbibed that passion for Irish melody which has never ceased to animate him since. It was well that the security of notation was so soon resorted to, for, even in 1809, at the time of the Editor's second publication, two only of the ten harpers assembled at Belfast on this occasion were surviving, and these two are long since dead. The meeting was attended by:

DENIS HEMPSON, (blind), from the County of Derry, aged 97 years.
ARTHUR O'NEILL, (blind), from the County of Tyrone, aged 58 years.
CHARLES FANNING, from the County of Caven, aged 56 years.
DANIEL BLACK, (blind), from the County of Derry, aged 75 years.
CHARLES BYRNE, from the County of Leitrim, aged 80.
HUGH HIGGINS, (blind), from the County of Mayo, aged 55.
PATRICK QUIN, (blind), from the County of Armagh, aged 47.
WILLIAM CARR, from the County of Armagh, aged 15.
ROSE MOONEY, (blind), from the County of Meath, aged 52.
JAMES DUNCAN, from the County of Down, aged 45.

advertise the festival and to invite all the best harpers to participate. A fund was set up to award prizes for excellence. Only ten harpers accepted the invitation; of these, six were blind and most all of them were aging.

A young pianist and organist, nineteen-year-old Edward Bunting, was appointed to record on paper the music that was played. For four days, the festival ensued "without the smallest interruption whatsoever, and each harper exerted himself to the utmost of their ability." The participants "played all Irish music," and were judged on their merits, with monetary awards being given to the performers. [48]

After describing the festival and listing the participants, Bunting goes on to list all the pieces played by each harper, along with comments on their appearance and manner of playing. The experience of recording the music of these aged harpers before they passed away, and the knowledge that the ancient music was passing with them, had an indelible effect on the young man. Four years after the Belfast Festival, Bunting published his first volume of the music he had written down: sixty-six melodies and several pages of introductory remarks on the history of the Irish harp. The title page of this publication, *A General Collection of the Ancient Irish Music*, describes its contents in lines of elaborate script, which read as follows:

1796 Bunting's first collection of Irish music

> "Containing a variety of Admired Aires
> never before published and also
> The Compositions of Conolan and Carolan
> Collected from the Harpers and in the different
> Provinces of Ireland
> and adapted for the Piano-Forte,
> with a Prefatory Introduction by Edward Bunting." [49]

Denis Hempson, Master of the Wire-Strung Harp

Denis Hempson was certainly one of the most remarkable harpers present at the Belfast Harp Festival, both because of his age, 97 years old, and because of his great expertise at playing the harp. Born a generation earlier than Turlough O'Carolan, Hempson was an accomplished performer and a master of the old Irish harp technique. As Bunting remarks about Hempson, "The pieces which he delighted to perform were unmixed with modern refinements, which he seemed studiously to avoid; confining himself chiefly to the most antiquated of those strains which have long survived the memory of their composers." [50]

1792 Denis Hempson, 97, plays at festival

Describing Hempson's proficiency upon the wire strings in the ancient manner, Bunting provides us with insight into the nature of his astonishing performance:

> Hempson was the only one of the harpers at the Belfast Meeting, in 1792, who literally played the harp with long crooked

nails, as described by the old writers. In playing he caught the string between the flesh and the nail; not like the other harpers of his day, who pulled it by the fleshy part of the fingers alone. He had an admirable method of playing Staccato and Legato, in which he could run through rapid divisions in an astonishing style. His fingers lay over the strings in such a manner, that when he struck them with one finger, the other was instantly ready to stop the vibration, so that the Staccato passages were heard in full perfection. [51]

In Hempson's playing, Bunting noticed the influence of the bardic tradition, seeing "vestiges of a noble system of practice that had existed for many centuries." On Hempson's exacting technique, Bunting writes, "When asked the reason of his playing certain parts of the tune or lesson in that style, his reply was, 'That is the way I learned it,' or, 'I cannot play it in any other.'" After extolling the accomplishments of Irish musical compostion and performance, Bunting concludes: "in fact, Hempson's Staccato and Legato passages, double slurs, shakes, turns, graces, etc., comprised as great a range of execution as has ever been devised by the most modern improvers." [52]

1807 Death of Hempson, master-harper

Denis Hempson lived to the remarkable old age of 112 years, retaining his mental faculties to the end of his life. He was said to have played his harp on the day before his death on November 5, 1807. Hempson's harp was the handsome instrument known as the Downhill Harp, poetically inscribed in 1702 by its maker, Cormac O'Kelly of County Derry. Today this harp is in the private collection of Arthur Guinness in Dublin. The inscription reads:

In the days of Noah I was green
After his flood I've not been seen
Until seventeen hundred and two, I was found,
By Cormac Kelly, under ground;
He raised me up to that degree,
Queen of Music they call me. [53]

Women Harpers in Buntings's Time

From the roster of harp players at the Belfast Festival, it can be seen that the harpers came generally from counties in the north and east of Ireland, that is, in the vicinity of Belfast. All the harpers were men except Rose Mooney of County Meath. Bunting notes that "although formerly it was very unusual for females to apply themselves to the harp," there were in fact two women at the time who had some reputation as performers in Ulster: Rose Mooney and another by the name of Catherine Martin, of Meath. [54] Little else is said about these harpers in Bunting's published volumes.

Considering the difficulty of travel at that time, it is likely that there were a number of harp players from other parts of the country who did not appear at the Festival. Some of these may have been women who could carry on the harping tradition in a modest fashion at home, or in the more secluded circumstances of the convent. Some may have played the harp with great proficiency, since little other education would have been available to them. A career as an traveling harper, however, would have been unthinkable.

From the harper Arthur O'Neill, we learn that Catherine Martin, or Kate, was born of poor parents in Lurgan, County Cavan and that she was nearly blind but could walk without a guide. O'Neill's account continues:

> She was taught the harp by a man named Owen Corr, with whom I had no acquaintance. Kate played very handsomely but had a strong partiality for playing the tunes composed by Parson Sterling   who was celebrated for his performance on the bagpipes. ... She seldom or never travelled out of the bounds of the County Cavan. [55]

In another account, O'Neill had, in his own words, "rambled into the County of Tyrone, where I fell in occasionally with different harpers." He goes on to say:

> I met my namesake Peggy O'Neill. ... She played decently on the harp. If fame don't tell lies of her, it mentioned that she was uncommon fond of playing all Carolan's planxties, such as 'Planxty Connor', 'Planxty Reilly', and about twenty-eight other planxties, which poor Peggy always set to music on her instrument on a C flat. [56]

On another visit to County Tyrone, at Ned Conway's near Newtown Stewart, O'Neill meets and shares tunes with a Miss Conway, "who played the harp uncommon well." In Dublin, O'Neill has a compliment for a Miss Ryan of Beresford Street, "who played very decently on the harp." [57]

Unlike some others, Rose Mooney did travel to various festivals, attended by a maid. From O'Neill's memoirs we learn that Rose Mooney was born in the County of Meath of unknown circumstances, that she was blind, and that she learned to play the harp from a shady character, Thady Elliott. We also learn from O'Neil that Rose Mooey earned third place at the Belfast Festival, her usual standing at such competitions.

Several women have been noted as harp teachers; Denis Hempson began his harp study at the age of twelve in 1707 with a teacher by the name of Bridget O'Cahan. And Hugh O'Neill, another of the traveling harpers, was taught by a woman named O'Sheil. Bunting quotes Hempson as saying: " 'in these old times, women as well as men were taught the Irish harp in the best families, and every Irish family had harps in plenty.' " [58] Though it is likely that Hempson is exaggerating about the number of harps in every home, in the old days the Irish harp may have been played as often by women as it was by men.

There are more bits and pieces in various memoirs and accounts. It does not appear that Bunting interviewed any women musicians in particular, but perhaps more research can yet be done to shed light on the lives of these women harpers.

EDWARD BUNTING COLLECTS THE ANCIENT MUSIC OF IRELAND

After his experience at Belfast, Edward Bunting made the study of the ancient music of his country and the preservation of the Irish melodies the main business of his life. After his first volume in 1796, he spent years traveling and listening to the music, writing notes and transcribing the melodies as he went. His accounts of his travels tell how he went "from one to another to note their repertoire of airs, with his ink-satchel and his little penny notebook." [59] Not himself a harp player, presumably Bunting set down the melodies he heard, then later edited the music, devising suitable bass parts to be played on the piano.

In 1809, under a title very similar to that of his first book, Edward Bunting published an expanded volume, *A General Collection of the Ancient Music of Ireland*. This work includes songs and a comprehensive essay on the history of the Irish harp and its predecessors. Bunting's third and final volume was published in 1840, three years before his death. This work, *The Ancient Music of Ireland*, also arranged for piano, included over 150 musical pieces collected from various sources, as well as a dissertation on the Trinity College Harp and Bunting's full account of the Belfast Festival and its participants.

1840 Bunting's complete "Ancient Music of Ireland"

TUNING THE HARP, TRANSCRIBING THE MUSIC

According to Bunting, the harpers of the Belfast Festival tuned their harps in a uniform manner, although they did not seem to know the origin of this practice. They also made use of the same set of terms for parts of their harps and their techniques of playing, suggesting a long tradition of playing in certain ways.

Bunting describes the tuning methods of these harpers and provides a diagram of the scale often used to tune a thirty-string harp (figure 21). However, in the process of writing

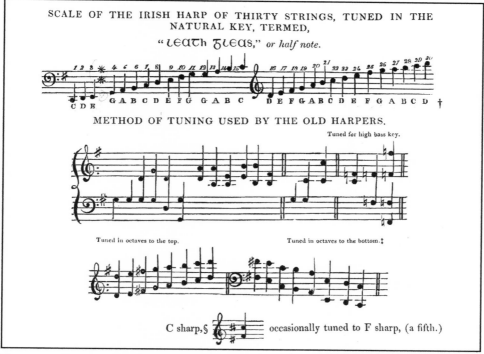

FIGURE 22. SCALE OF THE IRISH HARP, FROM BUNTING'S *ANCIENT MUSIC OF IRELAND*.

TUNING USED BY THE OLD HARPERS

As shown in the diagram above, from Bunting's *The Ancient Music of Ireland*, a harp of thirty strings was tuned diatonically from the C below the bass staff to the D above the treble staff. There is a notable omission of low F in the bass, while the upper three F's are raised to F#. Another unusual feature of the tuning method is the doubled G below middle C. When starting to tune the harp, these two strings, known to the Belfast harpers as "the Sisters," were the first to be tuned, in unison, to the proper pitch. The next string to be tuned was the D a fifth above the doubled G strings, and then the G one octave above that baseline position. Tuning would continue for the central strings by fifths and octaves, proceeding to the upper and the lower strings by octaves based on strings originally tuned, in a manner similar to that used by many present-day harpers.

This method of tuning, also favored by fiddlers, with F# in the treble, and no low F in the bass, allowed the Belfast harpers to play in the key of C major, the key of G major, and the corresponding minor keys.

Other modal scales were also used by these harpers. The use of the doubled G, about mid-scale, may have been a method for identifying a position on the harp for 18th century harpers, so many of whom were blind.

down the music he heard, in all editions of his music Bunting departed from the basic keys illustrated in the diagram and introduced other keys with as many as four flats or sharps. His written music gives the impression to the unsuspecting admirer of Irish music that it was customary for harpers of his day to play in many different keys. Such was not the case, for there were no levers nor mechanical devices on Irish harps played in 1792. The only method of altering pitch would have been to stop playing and re-tune the harp.

When Bunting was completing his 1840 edition, the Irish harps of that day would have had manual levers, but the music he published, designed as it was for piano, would still not have been convenient for playing on nineteenth century Irish harps. And while Bunting preserved many of Carolan's melodies, the rapidly repeated bass notes and accidentals were not likely to have been produced on Carolan's harp.

Bunting has been both revered for preserving Ireland's ancient music and reproached for altering the authentic music of the harpers to accommodate the piano. It is likely that the thought never occured to Bunting to do it any other way — it was the time when the old music, the smaller harps, and the ways of playing it were coming to an end.

As an invaluable record of the musical culture of Ireland, the contribution of Edward Bunting to the preservation of the Irish harp and the music of Ireland is important, not just for harp players, but for all musicians.

Irish Harp after the Belfast Festival

Following the Belfast Harp Festival and the publication of Bunting's first collection in 1796, a number of Harp Societies were established in both Dublin and Belfast, with expert teachers appointed to teach the instrument. A benevolent plan was begun to teach the harp to blind youths, so that they might

1796 Harp Societies in Belfast

make a career of harp playing, as Turlough O'Carolan and many others had done. This effort continued for some twenty years but was not very sucessful. Perhaps the participants lacked the essential musical gifts that had distinguished their famous predecessors.

Another problem was lack of proper instruments, "for making a true Irish harp was as special a skill as playing one, and city makers did not make them," notes Joan Rimmer in her summary comments near the end of her book, The Irish Harp. She goes on to express the dilemma:

> The instrument's big, sweet sonority and non-chromatic tuning were out of place in the musical world of the early eighteen-hundreds. While the harpers of sixteenth-century Ireland had been able to turn their aristocratic skills to other kinds of music when the old Gaelic world was burst apart, the eighteenth-century harpers, already archaic and somewhat anachronistic, could not adapt to the nineteenth century. By the end of that century's second decade the old Irish harp was gone. [60]

THE EXILED IRISH HARPERS

It is tempting to speculate on the influence of Irish harpers who were forced from their homeland by centuries of oppression. Of the harpers who were banished from Ireland during the later years of Queen Elizabeth's rule at the end of the 16th century, we know of one, Rory Dall O'Cathain, who was a member of a noble family of County Derry. After the Flight of the Earls in 1607, this blind harper lived mainly in Scotland, playing before King James VI of Scotland. Rory Dall O'Cathain composed the lovely air still played today, "O Give Me Your Hand," and died about 1650 at an extreme old age. Was it he who played the harps we know as the Lamont Harp and the Queen Mary Harp, so similar in form to the Trinity College Harp?

And what happened to the musicians who accompanied the nobles who left Ireland at the end of the 17th century during the Flight of the Wild Geese? And again, at the end of the 18th century in 1798, just a few years after the famous Belfast Festival, the people of Wexford rose up and were brutally crushed and defeated. Along with those who fled were there any Irish harpers who took themselves off to other parts of the British Isles, to France, or to elsewhere in Europe?

Considering the hopeful relationship of the Irish to the French, it may be that the French school of harp playing has been enriched through the centuries by Irish harpers who despaired of life in their native country. Certainly the classic repertoire for concert, or pedal harp has been served elegantly by French composers and French harpists. Excellent music for *Harpe Celtique* or *Harpe sans pedals* has been published in France today. The harp has been prominent as well in Spain and also in Italy, final resting place of the famous Irish earls, Hugh O'Neill and Rory O'Donnell.

The apparent disappearance of the old Irish harp that occurred around the beginning of the 19th century did not mean that the Irish harp was extinguished. The old harpers themselves may have died out, unknown and unappreciated. And the use and form of the harp became more obscure as public conditions and preferences changed, but it is probably more accurate to say that the old harp simply went out of the public view. Some harps surely survived in private homes or were cared for and played in the monasteries and convents. And memories of the harp surely lingered at the back of the minds of the Irish people.

c. 1800
Disappearance of Irish Harp?

John Egan's Royal Portable Harp

One effort by a harpmaker to provide an acceptable alternative for the Irish harp that had practically disappeared was that of John Egan and his "Royal Portable" harp. Early in the 19th century Egan, a Dublin harpmaker, began producing

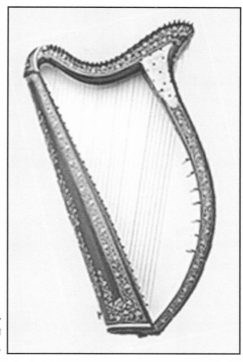

FIGURE 23. EGAN'S ROYAL PORTABLE HARP, DUBLIN, 1819. THREE FEET TALL, WITH SEVEN FINGER LEVERS, OR "DITALS" TO CHANGE PITCH.

harps that differed significantly from the traditional sturdy Irish harps with the one-piece soundbox. The harps Egan produced, though small in size, took on the lines and construction of the pedal harps patented by Sebastion Erard in 1810 that had been appearing in France and England. Some of the earlier harps made by Egan were wire-strung with thin brass or steel but they did not have a good tone and were not successful.

1819
Egan designs
Portable
Irish Harp

The "Royal Portable," a new design produced by Egan in 1819 did become popular for a while. [61] This small harp had mechanical features resembling those of the pedal harp, but it was only three feet high and designed to be carried about, as Irish harps always had been. Instead of pedals to alter the pitch, this harp had seven small finger levers, or ditals, set into the hollowed but traditionally bowed forepillar. Moving the levers activated disks mounted in the neck above each string, so that all the strings of one note would change key at the same time. For example, all the F strings would change to F# with one turn of a lever, in the manner of the pedal-operated, string-shortening devices built in to the column of the large pedal harp. An example of the Egan Portable Harp can be seen today in the Metropolitan Museum of Art, New York, in the Crosby Brown Collection of 1889.

1889
Egan harp to Metropolitan Museum

Egan's complicated key-change mechanism, involving the hands to turn levers instead of the feet to move pedals, did not last. This small hybrid harp was a good attempt to answer the desire for pitch change in a portable harp, but although these harps were enjoyed for a while by the wealthy, they fell out of fashion and did not survive. And, by the mid-nineteenth century, Ireland was so badly devastated by the Great Famine and the disrupted social system that the bare struggle for existence allowed little leisure or means for harpmaking or harp playing.

One improvement Egan made on his small harp did have a lasting effect on the concept of what an "Irish harp" could be. Egan used gut strings (from sheep) instead of the traditional metal strings for his Portable Harp, which greatly improved the tone. The softer strings helped avoid the excessive vibration of the pitch-changing mechanisms.

A full century later Egan's altered form for a harp of Ireland, his Portable Harp, would be copied and manufactured by Melville Clark in the United States, with an improved and much simpler blade action for changing the pitch of the strings. Although sometimes termed the "neo-Irish" harp to distinguish it from the likes of Brian Boru's ancient instrument, this style of harp became known in the 20th century as the "Irish Harp."

Chapter 8
Irish Loss, Survival,
and a New Spirit
Late 19th and Early 20th Centuries

Chapter 8~ Irish Loss, Survival, and a New Spirit
Late 19th and Early 20th Centuries

Late Nineteenth Century

1845   *Famine begins, a million die*

1846   *Irish start emigration to America*

1856   *Royal Irish Academy of Music founded*

1893   *Formation of the Gaelic League*

Early Twentieth Century

1902   *MacFall "Tara" harp designed*

1904   *Abbey Theatre founded*

1903   *R.B. Armstrong's "The Irish and the Highland Harps"*

1919   *Irish War of Independence*

1922   *Formation of the Irish Free State*

1926   *Design of the new Irish coinage*

1845-1848
The Great
Famine

After John Egan created a small portable harp in the early nineteenth century, there is little to say about the development of the harp in Ireland in the ensuring years, which were tragic beyond measure. The potato blight of 1845 to 1846 wiped out the principal source of sustenance for a large part of the Irish population. Without reviewing the deplorable reasons for this, it is sufficient to say that starvation and disease took mortal toll —a million people died— and hundreds of thousands of Irish were forced to leave their homeland in order to survive. In the ensuing emigration, thousands fled to Britain and even greater numbers surged across the Atlantic to America in a steady stream for the next fifty years, reducing Ireland's population by half.

Those who survived the crossing landed in Boston or New York, establishing Irish communities in these cities. Many moved southward to Philadelphia, westward to the industrial centers of Detroit and Chicago, or northward to Montreal and Toronto, where they had to work at the most menial of jobs to support themselves. Gangs of Irishmen worked on building the railroads, keeping up their spirits with song and drink, giving a particular Irish flavor to the history of that westward expansion. All brought their memories of home and separation, most with old tunes in their hearts. Some of the more fortunate brought a fiddle or other small instrument from home but these Irish workers left scant record of the harp.

Dispersion of the Irish following the famine was a terrible loss for Ireland. In a way, however, it was a gain for the rest of the world, an enrichment of the places where the Irish settled. Besides the United States, the Irish emigrated to Australia, New Zealand, and Canada, all countries where an Irish influence is still strongly felt.

The most grievous loss to the culture of Ireland was the near passing of Gaelic, its traditional language. All aspects of Irish culture suffered along with the suffering population, but as Giovanni Costigan explains:

> The famine still further weakened the declining hold of the Gaelic language upon the Irish people. For its ravages had been most severe, the emigration most concentrated, in those areas of the west and southwest where the majority of Gaelic speakers had lived. As Douglas Hyde put it, in the years after the Famine, the language 'just wilted off the face of Ireland.' Between 1861 and 1891, except in certain districts of the Gaelteacht, the old language died out almost completely. In 1891, according to Dr. Hyde, there were fewer Gaelic speakers in all Ireland than there had been before the Famine in the single province of Connacht. [62]

Irish traditional music, song, and dance dwindled as well. Little wonder that the Irish harp went mute.

✳ ✳ ✳ ✳

From this depth, positive change came very slowly. In 1893 Douglas Hyde, later to become the first president of independent Eire, founded the Gaelic League for the purpose of preserving and restoring Ireland's native language. William Butler Yeats appeared during this time of need with a great outcry, inspiring what became known as the Irish Literary Revival. With Lady Augusta Gregory, in 1904 Yeats founded the Abbey Theatre, which would become an intellectual center for the spirit of Ireland's rebirth. [63]

1893 Gaelic League founded

Irish nationalism finally erupted in rebellion on April 16, 1916, ignited by the passions of a gentle schoolmaster, Patrick H. Pearse, author of The Easter Proclamation of 1916. This famous document begins: "In the name of God and of the dead generations from which she receives her old tradition of nationhood, Ireland, through us, summons her children to her flag and strikes for her freedom." Within three weeks all seven

1916 Easter Rising

signers of the Proclamation were shot. Ireland rose, but it would take two world wars and another whole generation before the Republic of Ireland was proclaimed on April 18, 1949, severing a bondage of eight hundred years.

PRESERVATION OF THE IRISH HARP AND ITS MUSIC

Along with the language, the Gaelic cultural revival sparked interest in Irish traditional music and instruments. A major work produced around the turn of the century and first published in 1904 was *The Irish and The Highland Harps* by Robert Bruce Armstrong. Armstrong, of Scottish origin, spent many years researching the material for this important study. This extraordinary book, full of meticulous drawings by the author and others, and including photographs, is a masterpiece of information about the early Irish and Scottish harps. It remains the definitive study on the subject, and is much favored with harpmakers for its detailed illustrations and harp specifications.

1904
The Irish and the Highland Harps

While Armstrong was studying harps in Scotland and Ireland, in the United States, Captain Francis O'Neill, Chief of Police in Chicago, preserved Irish music in a monumental 1903 collection titled *The Music of Ireland*. From Tralibane, County Cork, O'Neill was born near the end of the Great Famine and left Ireland at the age of sixteen. After traveling the world as a seaman, in 1873 O'Neill signed on as a Chicago policeman. With the memory of songs from his childhood, Captain O'Neill went to great lengths to uncover Irish traditional music and those who could play it. He would travel the streets of Chicago, listening to the humming and whistling of tunes, and then go back and play the melodies on his flute before writing them down. Included in the thousands of songs collected from ordinary people and traditional musicians are over seventy

1903
Captain O'Neill, The Music of Ireland

tunes of Turlough O'Carolan, the eighteenth-century Irish harper. [64]

In Ireland itself, playing of the Irish harp, although diminished by the end of the 19th century, was carried on by sisters in the convents. One in particular, Sister M. Attracta Coffey of Loreto Abbey, was a distinguished musician well known in Ireland and England as a harpist of great talent. In 1903, Sister Attracta collected and published a *Tutor for the Irish Harp*, as well as two subsequent books of Irish melodies. Sister Attracta, later Mother Attracta Coffey, passed away at Loreto Abbey in 1920. Her successor, Mother Alphonsus O'Connor, would in turn teach many other harpists in Ireland, including Sheila Cuthbert, whose 1975 publication, *The Irish Harp Book*, incorporated the work of Sister Attracta.

1903
Tutor for the Irish Harp

THE MACFALL "TARA HARP"

In 1902, a harp was made in Belfast that became the prototype for a new style of an Irish harp, influencing a number of other harpmakers in Ireland. The "Tara Harp," made by James MacFall for Cardinal Logue, had a soundbox shaped like that of the pedal harp, with a rounded back. The head of the harp was high, with a bowed forepillar, and the harp was set upon little feet. A device for raising the pitch was mounted in the neck above each string; at the time these pins were known as "blades." Strings were a combination of gut in the treble and fine wire in the bass. The entire MacFall Tara harp was elaborately decorated with Celtic designwork.

1902
MacFall-Tara Harp

TRADITIONAL IRISH HARP EMERGES FROM OBSCURITY

Grass roots musical efforts and the work of a small circle of dedicated harpists nurtured the growth of the Irish harp from early in the twentieth century through the 1940s. One colorful

FIGURE 24. THE TARA HARP MADE BY
JAMES MACFALL OF BELFAST IN 1902.

tale is of Treasa Ní Chormaic, who, as one of the few true descendents of the old harpers was taught harp by her father and said to have played an old harp found in a bog.[65]

Early 1900s Teaching of Irish Harp begins

Other sources mention Caroline Townshend, daughter of an eminent philanthropist in nineteenth century Irish life, who "…set herself the task of rediscovering the long since outlawed Irish harp, the emblem of Ireland. After much research and looking she found one in Wales. She then gave free lessons and many copies of her harp were made." [66] Among her early harp students were Máirín Ní Shé and her sister Róisín Ní Shé, who became renowned harpists and teachers of the Irish harp in the mid-twentieth century. Sheila Cuthbert notes that Caroline Townshend was "…interested in everything Irish, the language, culture, music, and she taught the Irish Harp to anyone interested, especially to the local girls near her home…in Dublin, she was delighted to find herself teaching

105

quite advanced musicians…the O'Shea sisters and many others." [67]

✳ ✳ ✳ ✳

In addition to the work of individuals, a number of educational institutions in Ireland have long offered Irish harp instruction, encouraging the preservation and growth of the harp and Irish music. In Dublin, two notable Catholic institutions that have taught harp for many years are Loreto Abbey at Rathfarnmham, and the Dominican Convent at Sion Hill, Blackrock, where Máirín Ní Shé taught harp for many years.

Musical instruction of all kinds, including Irish harp, has long been available at the Royal Irish Academy of Music (R.I.A.M.), a major Irish institution founded in 1856. The RIAM has long been known for its rigorous examination requirements in harp and other instruments. Current-day studies in Irish harp at this academy include eight grades of study and a required repertoire of performance pieces arranged by well-known Irish harpists. [68]

✳ ✳ ✳ ✳

Sister Angela Walshe, who taught music at Sion Hill Convent since the 1930s and was Head of Music there for many years, had been intensely devoted to the revival of the Irish harp, and did what she could to find harps to use in teaching. An interesting anectdote tells how this persistent nun obtained the harps she needed while inspiring the establishment of a sucessful business, Quinn Harps.

John Quinn, an expert craftsman, had maintained a musical instrument repair shop on the premises of the Royal Irish Academy of Music for many years where his family had been employed ever since the RIAM was established in the mid-nineteenth century. John Quinn would occasionally repair harps along with other instruments for the teachers at the Academy and other nearby institutions, including Sion Hill.

FIGURE 25. QUINN HARP MADE IN 1974, 43 INCHES TALL , 23 INCHES WIDE ON FOUR SMALL FEET. THIRTY-ONE STRINGS, WITH FIVE LOWER OF WOUND WIRE, OTHERS OF THIN GUT. LARGE BRASS BLADES SET IN THE NECK FOR CHANGING PITCH.

FIGURES26. WALTONS' "CELTIC HARP." MADE IN 1970S. HARP IS ABOUT 47 INCHES TALL, WITH NYLON STRINGS AND SHARPING LEVERS.

With so few harps available, Sister Angela would prevail upon Quinn to accept harps for repair that were long past their best and needed considerable skill and effort to restore. The idea for the Quinn Harp was born one day in the late thirties, when Sister Angela sent to John what John later described to his brother Patrick as a "bag of bits" to repair. John had remarked at the time that it would be easier to just make a new harp than to repair that collection of junk! With her usual charm, Sister Angela had challenged John to do just that. [69]

John Quinn worked many years to get his design the way he wanted, finally starting production in the mid 1940s. Quinn Harps were sold widely in Ireland, the United States, and Europe from the 1940s up until the 1970s.

1940s
John Quinn
designs
harps

✵ ✵ ✵ ✵

Founded in 1922 during the rise of Irish Nationalism, Waltons Musical Instrument Galleries of Dublin has been involved in promoting the revival of Gaelic culture, particularly Irish traditional music. As instrument makers as well as music publishers, Waltons has produced a number of Irish-style harps since the early 1960s. In the 1970s, Waltons' "Celtic Harp," elaborately hand carved and painted, was designed to combine aspects of the large concert harp along with the small harps as played in Ireland in earlier centuries.

IRISH-STYLE HARPS MADE IN THE UNITED STATES

In the early years of the twentieth century, a harpmaker in Syracuse, New York began to give serious attention to the production of Irish-style harps. By 1913, Melville Clark had designed and produced an Irish harp design that was similar in appearance to the 1819 Egan Portable Harp, created a century before. The harp has 31 strings, stands 39 inches high, and can be raised to a height of 52 inches using the folding stand. Well over one thousand of the Clark Irish harps were

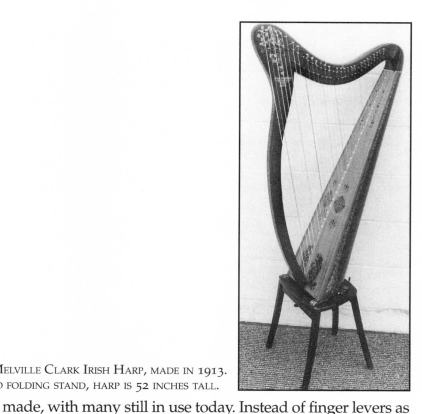

FIGURE 27. MELVILLE CLARK IRISH HARP, MADE IN 1913.
ATTACHED TO FOLDING STAND, HARP IS 52 INCHES TALL.

*1913 -1950
Clark Irish
harps*

made, with many still in use today. Instead of finger levers as on the Egan harp, Clark used a blade system that was simpler to install and more practical to play. Melville Clark harps were made up until the 1950s when Mr. Clark passed away and his company changed hands. His well-made harps were very popular and were shipped all over the world.

THE HARP ON THE IRISH COINS

*1926
New Irish
Coinage
Designed*

In 1922, after the years of struggle in the Irish War of Independence, the Irish Free State was formed, and occasion arose for the creation of a complete set of coinage for the new nation. William Butler Yeats, poet and statesman, was chairman of the committee set up by the Irish Government in 1926 to give advice on the designing of an Irish coinage. The committee decided that a harp should appear on all of the new coins, as it had on Ireland's early coins, and that the image should be

FIGURE 28. IRISH COINS, FROM TOP, LEFT TO RIGHT: THE HALFCROWN, A HORSE (1964); THE FLORIN, A SALMON (1954); THE PENNY, A HEN WITH CHICKS (1968); AND THE MORBIDUCCI PATTERN SHILLING DESIGN (1926).

that of the Trinity College Harp. Seven artists were commissioned and each was to submit a set of designs within the given themes. [65] After careful consideration of designs from a distinguished selection of international artists, the committee chose the work of an English artist, Percy Metcalfe. Back-to-back, upon the coins, with appealing likenesses of the birds and beasts of Ireland, is a handsome image of the Trinity College Harp.

Although the Irish coinage have been redesigned over the years, the Euro coin issued in Ireland in 2001 still carries an image of this ancient harp. Tiny silver and copper harps passing daily through the hands of all her people are a mute reminder, to those who notice, of Ireland's heritage.

Chapter 9
Mid-Twentieth Century
Revival of the Irish Harp
In Ireland and Around the World

Chapter 9 ~ Mid-Twentieth Century Revival of the Irish Harp In Ireland and Around the World

1930s Irish harps played at Celtic Congresses

Post World War II

1949   Founding of the Repulic of Ireland

1951   First Fleadh Cheoil na hEireann

           Founding of Comhaltas Ceoltóirí Éireann

1953   First An Tóstal, "Ireland at Home" Festival

1957   Mary O'Hara's Songs of Erin

1958   "Carolan, the Life and Times"

           by Donal O'Sullivan

1960   Founding of Cairde na Cruite

1961   Restoration of Trinity College Harp

Nineteen Seventies

1971   Stivell's "Renaissance de la Harpe Celtique"

1972   Derek Bell joins The Cheiftains

1975   Sheila Cuthbert's "The Irish Harp Book"

With the end of World War II in 1945, the efforts of those interested in the revival of the Gaelic language, music, and culture gradually emerged. Radio Éireann, which had been broadcasting since the days of the Irish Free State in the 1920s, continued its work of promoting a national Irish identity. In 1948, the Radio Éireann Symphony Orchestra was established with a principal harpist among its members. The following year, the Republic of Ireland was formally established, along with the painful reality that Northern Ireland would remain part of Great Britain. Music and art knew no boundaries, and promotion of Irish culture continued, advanced by a number of dedicated individuals, groups, and organizations.

✳ ✳ ✳ ✳

The promotion of Irish culture, or more generally Celtic culture, was certainly not new in the 1950s. Celtic Congresses had been held regularly since 1917 in countries such as Scotland and Wales, with one or more harpists among the regular performers. These gatherings focused on political and educational methods to promote and support the use of Celtic languages. Traditional music and instruments were integral to this effort.[71] At the 1917 meeting of the Celtic Congress, held at Birkenhead, Wales, the reception included Scottish pipers, a harpist, and vocalists to entertain the guests. The 1930 Celtic Congress, the first ever to be held in London, opened with a concert of Celtic music by harpist Gwendolyn Mason. And around 1939, Irish harpist Róisín Ní She began performing regularly at these events. Along with advocates of using Gaelic, the original Celtic language in Ireland, a number of

Irish traditional musicians were determined to bring out what they knew to be the true sounds of the music of their country.

Before the 1950s, however, what was considered acceptable as "Irish music" was not necessarily the traditional music of the Irish countryside. The music of the ordinary people was not appreciated in some social circles, and although there were thousands of traditional musicians playing across Ireland, they kept a low profile. In 1951, however, the first *Fleadh Cheoil na hEireann* (Festival of Irish Music) was organized by the musicians themselves. From this gathering came the founding of Comhaltas Ceoltoiri Éireann that same year, an organization dedicated to promoting Irish culture. Though not well attended in the first years, by 1956 *Fleadh Cheoil na hEireann* had become a great national festival of traditional musicians, singers, and dancers from all parts of Ireland and overseas. [72]

1951 founding of Comhaltas Ceoltoiri Éireann

The Irish government recognized the appeal of the traditional arts, and introduced a festival celebrating Irish culture to be held in the spring of 1953 for the purpose of promoting commerce and attracting tourism. This event, *An Tóstal*, Irish for gathering or spectacle, was first held for a three-week period in April 1953. To honor the event, a commemorative stamp, symbolizing ancient Irish Festivals, was issued with a design of a stylized Irish harp (figure 29).

1953 First "Ireland at Home" Festival

An Tóstal events were held all over Ireland that first year, 1953. In Limerick, for example, music recitals, concerts, and a historical pageant were held along with spectacular sights such as 400 children from local dancing schools performing in unison a traditional Irish dance. [73] In Dublin, Máirín Ní Shé presented her Irish harp students, who were enthusiastically received and invited to perform on BBC radio and television. Among these students was the young singer Mary O'Hara, who by that time had been performing live on radio and would record her first album, *Songs of Erin*, three years later in 1957.

FIGURE 29 "AN TOSTAL" STAMP, FEBRUARY 9TH, 1953 AND FIRST DAY OF ISSUE DESIGN: IRISH "GREEN FLAG" WITH HISTORIC HARP IN FRONT OF THE FLAG OF IRELAND.

A cultural event that linked Ireland and America was the 1956 tour of cities in the United States and Canada by the Irish Festival Singers, with Sheila Larchet as their harpist playing Irish traditional music. Two years later, in 1958, the two-volume biography of Turlough O'Carolan by Dr. Donal O'Sullivan appeared, a landmark event in the study of Irish music. This comprehensive work provided, for the first time, the details needed to understand the life, the poetry, and the history of this most important Irish musician, as well as a notation of the melodies. Dr. O'Sullivan's work was an inspiration to many, providing a foundation for those interested in studying the Irish harp and its music.

For those who wanted to play the harp in Ireland, however, there were only a few teachers in the 1950s and 1960s for either the concert-style pedal harp or the smaller Irish harp. Along with few teachers, there were very few harps to be had. Any attempts at large-scale production of harps in Ireland had been suspended during the war years; some independent harpmakers were active, but no harps were made in any number.

In the United States, Melville Clark had been making his version of an Irish harp since 1911. Clark pioneered the use of nylon strings for small harps in 1948, and many of his harps came to be used in Ireland during the 1950s. Susan Reed, singing songs of the British Isles accompanied by her Clark Irish harp, helped to popularize the instrument in the United States.

Instrument makers in Ireland, Scotland, and other countries also started building harps to meet the growing interest in a revived Irish harp, sometimes called the neo-Irish harp to distinguish it from the ancient Irish harp. In Japan, the Aoyama Company began building a harp similar to the Melville Clark Irish harp and beginning in the early 1960s, Aoyama shipped many harps to Ireland and the United States. Large company harpmakers in the United States, such as Lyon & Healy, also began making alternatives to the pedal harp in the 1960s. However, until nearly two decades later, good, commercially-made small harps continued to be very hard to find, both in Ireland and the United States.

✳ ✳ ✳ ✳

*1948
First use of
nylon harp
strings*

Besides the interest in harps for general use, independent craftspeople in several Celtic countries were working to create replicas of the ancient, historic harps, those played with long fingernails by the old-style harpers and seen now only in museums. Many musicians, musicologists, and composers were seeking an instrument that would allow them to recreate the much older and essentially Gaelic or Celtic music. In Brittany, the Celtic land in the north of France, harpmaker Jord Cochevelou had been active since the 1930s in recreating the Breton wire-strung harp. His son, Alan Stivell, began playing a wire-strung Breton harp as a youth in the 1950s, and would later become an important innovator with this style of harp.

In Ireland, the one existing example of the ancient Irish harp, the legendary harp of Brian Boru, was not displayed in a true manner until after 1961. That year, the British Museum repaired and refurbished this treasure, which is now kept in the library at Trinity College in Dublin. At the time, several harpists and others in Ireland were allowed to briefly handle and play the instrument, newly strung with brass strings; this event no doubt contributed to the rising interest in the Irish harp at the time.

By 1965, the importance of the Irish harp and the music that could be played upon it was becoming recognized in Ireland, fostered by the Irish harp society Cairde na Cruite (friends of the harp). In 1960, this group of pioneering musicians set out to "revive the long dormant interest in the Irish Harp,"[74] and in 1965 asked Sheila Cuthbert to begin the compilation of a major study of the harp of Ireland. Ten years later when the study was near completion, this small harp and its music was on its way to a full-fledged renaissance.

Derek Bell, who will long be remembered as the harpist with the Chieftains, the group that brought Irish music to the world stage, had a brass-strung Irish harp made in the late 1960s. Already an accomplished oboist, composer, and pianist, Bell turned his attention to what he called the "Baroque Irish harp," experimenting with live radio performances of Irish airs played on the brass-strung harp with Baroque orchestra. When Derek Bell later joined the Chieftains in 1972, he brought his classical background to the playing of both the "neo-Irish" harp with gut or nylon strings, and the newly resurrected wire-strung, or old-style "authentic Irish" harp.

✳ ✳ ✳ ✳

Sean Ó Riada, later to become one of Ireland's most influential composers, grew up surrounded by traditional fiddlers in the countryside of Ireland, and was a strong advocate of restoring the Gaelic language. [75] By the early sixties, Ó Riada had produced Irish traditional music for films and plays, and very much wanted to use an authentic Irish harp in his work, expressing regret that the instrument he wished to compose for no longer existed outside the museum. At the time, only a few harpmakers in Ireland were working at creating a replica of such a harp. By the end of that decade, Rev. C.B. Warren, a Dublin clergyman, inspired by the work of Sean Ó Riada and others, hollowed out the trunk of a willow tree and created such a harp. Though not the first harpmaker to use this construction method, Warren's plans were the first to be made widely available through the pages of a new voice in folk music, the *Folk Harp Journal*. In 1974, Roland L. Robinson, founder and editor, printed Warren's contribution in Vol. 7 of his new magazine, which drew upon harp traditions from South America, various Celtic lands, and elsewhere in the world to nourish an emerging folk harp movement.

1974
Folk Harp
Journal

By 1975, Sheila Cuthbert's collection, *The Irish Harp Book, A Tutor and Companion*, appeared with its important mingling of contributions by classically trained composers, as well as pieces in the older, native-Irish style. In his foreword to the book, Brendan Breathnach, renowned folklorist, speaks of how this work goes far toward bridging barriers that had existed, particularly in Ireland, between "art" music and folk music. In 1975, he made a hopeful prediction:

1975
The Irish
Harp Book

> The present cultivation of the Irish harp has been sustained too long to be dismissed as an ephemeral interest in things of the past. It is not too fanciful, then, to see in it a nucleus from which will develop a national school of harping with a distinctive national style. [76]

Not only did the work of Sheila Cuthbert, Mary O'Hara, Derek Bell, and many others do just that — promote a large-scale revival of the Irish harp in their native country — in addition, interest in this harp spread across the globe. More than a national school of harping, an international interest in playing small harps has continued to grow beyond what such artists may ever have imagined.

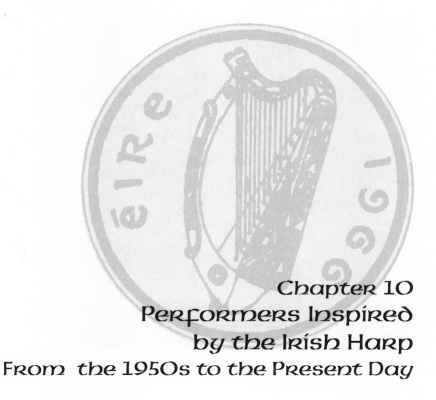

Chapter 10
Performers Inspired
by the Irish Harp
From the 1950s to the Present Day

Chapter 10 ~Performers Inspired by the Irish Harp From the 1950s to the Present Day

Máirín Ní Shé and Róisín Ní Shé

Mercedes Bolger and Gráinne Yeats

Nancy Calthorpe

Sheila Larchet Cuthbert

Mary O'Hara

Derek Bell

Janet Harbison

Máire Ní Chathasaigh

Gráinne Hambly

Ann Heymann

W e turn next to some notable performers, teachers, and harp players who have been influenced and inspired in their work by various forms of an Irish harp. Not a comprehensive listing of all the artists that might be mentioned, nor necessarily those most important in the complete history of the Irish harp, the artists here represent a selection of those involved. Several personal memoirs have been added with impressions and reflections about some of the musicians.

Máirín Ní Shé and Róisín Ní Shé

Máirín Ní Shé and her sister Róisín Ní Shé[77] first learned to play the Irish harp when young from Caroline Townsend and later went on to other studies, becoming renowned harpists and performers. As a performer, Máirín Ní Shé won many awards for singing and harp playing, representing Ireland as a harpist internationally. Máirín Ní Shé also taught harp and singing for many years as a member of the music faculty at the Dominican Convent at Sion Hill, Dublin, introducing student harpists to the Irish public in 1953 at the newly revived Irish music festival, *An Tóstal*. At the time Máirín was invited to London to lecture on the subject of the Irish harp, where her work was enthusiastically received. Máirín Ní Shé was honored by many of her current and former pupils in 1978 at her Silver Jubilee, celebrating twenty-five years of teaching Irish Harp at Sion Hill.

Róisín Ní Shé became an internationally known harpist and lecturer, performing as Harper-Singer at many Inter-Celtic Congresses held during the years 1939 to 1969 in Brittany, Wales, Cornwall, Scotland, and the Isle of Man.[78] Róisín Ní

FIGURE 30: IRISH HARP STUDENTS OF MÁIRÍN NÍ SHÉ AT SION HILL CONVENT, DUBLIN, 1978. EACH HARP IS SLIGHTLY DIFFERENT.

MEETING MÁIRÍN AND RÓISÍN NÍ SHÉ IN 1978

During a visit to Dublin in September of 1978, I met both Máirín and Róisín Ní Shé. Róisín and her family entertained me in their home, with Róisín singing and playing traditional airs on her original McFall Tara harp while her son played the flute. At Sion Hill Convent, Máirín and her pupils entertained me with singing accompanied by their Irish harps, with everyone seated around in an informal harp circle. I noticed that they all sat beside their instruments with the harp on their right side as I had seen Mary O'Hara do. A harp was passed around for everyone to play in turn and when it came to me, I straddled the harp as is customary when playing the pedal harp. I heard a few giggles from the girls and the teacher's "hush." I went ahead and played for them "Miss MacDemott, or the Princess Royal," a Carolan tune that I had learned at home from Nancy Calthorpe's first small volume. Máirín and her students clapped enthusiastically, appreciating my interest in their instrument and music. I asked the girls to sit with their harps, and took this picture of them in front of the wall full of harp notices and events.

— NJC

FIGURE 31: MÁIRÍN NÍ SHÉ
PLAYING HER ORIGINAL McFALL
TARA HARP, 1978.

Shé also performed widely on radio and television and at many
Irish music and language festivals. Both Máirín and Róisín Ní
Shé were proficient at the art of singing while at the same
time playing the harp, a skill known as singing to one's own
harp accompaniment. Awards are given for this art, and at
one festival, the *Feis Ceoil*, Róisín was named "Gold Medalist
for Irish Traditional Singing." [79]

MERCEDES BOLGER AND GRÁINNE YEATS

Two notable harpists, early members of Cairde na Cruite and
known in Ireland since the 1950s as performers and arrangers
of Irish music, are Mercedes Bolger and Gráinne Yeats. In 1969,
these two harpists played the premier preformance of *Introduction and Air for Two Harps*, a composition by Joan Trimble
that had been comissioned at the time by Cairde na Cruite.[80]
For many years, Gráinne Yeats served as the chair of this important harp society.

Mercedes Bolger, a prominent concert harpist, was Professor of Harp for some years at the Royal Irish Academy of
Music (RIAM), and was a teacher of harp to Mary O'Hara in
the 1950s. Studying cello and harp as a youth, Miss Bolger

123

(later Mrs. Garvey), recorded Irish music in various countries of Europe, and performed as a concert harpist in Ireland. [81] Mercedes Bolger made many arrangements of Irish music and in the 1990s collaborated with Gráinne Yeats on the music collection *Sounding Harps.*

Starting her career as a singer, Gráinne Yeats learned Irish songs in the Gaelteacht areas of Ireland where she has spent much time. Mrs. Yeats first heard a harp about 1950, found a second hand Scottish harp to play, and learned basic harp technique from Sheila Cuthbert and Mercedes Bolger. Not too much later, Gráinne Yeats found herself teaching harp at the R.I.A.M., even though she didn't feel extremely well-qualified for the position — there were simply no other harp teachers available. [82]

With a long-time interest in the wire-strung harp, Gráinne Yeats has made recordings using several styles of harps. Her 1992 book, *The Harp of Ireland*, focuses on the Belfast Harp Festival of 1792, a critical point in the history of Irish music.

NANCY CALTHORPE

Born in 1914, a native of Waterford, Nancy Calthorpe comes from a family of professional musicians associated with the musical life of that area for over a century. From an early age she studied music, first in Ireland, then in London and on the Continent. Along with her academic degrees, Nancy Calthorpe studied singing and Irish harp with both Sheila Cuthbert and Máirín Ní Shé. Miss Calthorpe taught all aspects of harp and music at both the Loreto Abbey and Sion Hill Convents, as well as at other musical institutions and colleges. She also acted as Adjudicator at all the leading Irish Festivals, and in 1966 was awarded a major prize, *An Oireachtas*, for her setting of "Three Irish songs to Irish Harp Accompaniment."

FIGURE 32. EXCERPT FROM "MUSIC FOR THE IRISH HARP, A TRIBUTE TO O'CAROLAN," BY NANCY CALTHORPE, 1969.

FIGURE 33. NANCY CALTHORPE, IN THE DOORWAY TO HER HOME IN DUBLIN AT FITZWILLIAM SQUARE WITH ITS DISTINCTIVE WINDOWS. OCT 1978.

In 1970, anticipating the 300th anniversary of the birth of Turlough O'Carolan (1670 – 1738), Miss Calthorpe created and personally published a small collection of ten Carolan airs nicely arranged for Irish Harp, *Music for the Irish Harp, A Tribute to O'Carolan*. [83] At that time a special observance of Carolan's birth and life was held, presided over by the notable harpist Gwendolyn Mason. [84]

In 1974 the publication of a larger work, *The Calthorpe Collection, Songs and Airs Arranged for the Voice and Irish Harp*, was the occasion for a handsome reception in Dublin given by Allied Irish Banks, sponsors of the publication. Many of Ireland's leading artists contributed to a concert for this occasion. Nancy Calthorpe passed away in 1998 and is remembered as a respected harp teacher, and for her work as a collector and publisher of music for the Irish harp, still widely used today.

SHEILA LARCHET CUTHBERT

Sheila Larchet Cuthbert, author of *The Irish Harp Book, a Tutor and Companion*, comes from a distinguished family of Irish musicians. Receiving her early musical education from her parents, both eminent musicians, she also studied piano and cello at the Royal Irish Academy of Music. Sheila's father, Dr. John F. Larchet, composer and conductor, was Director of Music at the Abbey Theatre during its heyday, from 1907 to 1934.

Sheila Larchet began her harp studies with Mother Alphonsus O'Conner, who succeeded Mother Attracta Coffey as harpist at Loreto Abbey, Rathfarnham, Dublin, and then continued professional study with harpist Tina Bonifacio in England. After obtaining her academic degrees, Sheila spent two years as principal harpist with the Liverpool Philharmonic Orchestra before returning to Dublin in 1948 to become the first permanent harpist with the newly established Radio Éireann Symphony Orchestra (RÉSO). At the time and into the 1950s, outside the cities of Dublin and Belfast, there were no other professional orchestras in Ireland at all. [85]

In 1955, an opportunity arose for Sheila to tour the United States as harpist-accompanist with the Irish Festival Singers, a twelve-voice choir. Leaving the Radio Éireann orchestra, Sheila undertook the four-month tour of the United States and Canada and met her future husband, James Cuthbert, an accomplished vocalist with the choir. On returning to Ireland, Sheila continued teaching and playing both the pedal harp and the Irish harp. In 1958, Sheila Cuthbert collaborated with Donal O'Sullivan on a series of programs for Radio Éireann, requiring the creation of numerous arrangements of the music of Turlough O'Carolan and other early harpers. That same year, 1958, Dr. O'Sullivan, an eminent authority on Irish folk music, published his two-volume study, *Carolan, The Life Times and Music of an Irish Harper*, which includes music to over two hundred of Carolan's pieces.

In 1965, the Irish Harp Society Cairde na Cruite, responding to the severe need for suitable printed music for the Irish harp, appointed Sheila Cuthbert to compile and edit a new book on the subject. Appearing in 1975, *The Irish Harp Book* is a substantial book, beautifully printed in conventional music typeface, with accompanying historical, biographical, and technical data. An informative pre-publication description of the book was written by Mrs. Cuthbert, and is here reproduced with her permission.

Divided into twelve lessons, the book includes technical studies and exercises preliminary to selected pieces that provide music of increasing difficulty and historical perspective. Each lesson also includes pertinent music theory for the harpist with key structures, scales, chord, and arpeggio forms. An

The Irish Harp Book ~a tutor and companion

by Sheila Larchet Cuthbert

THE AUTHOR WRITES:

In planning this book, I conceived the idea of a comprehensive course of study, which would serve a student from the initial stage, to the most advanced music, from beginner to performer, in fact. It is important to remember that the Irish harp is a limited field: limited diatonically (by reason of the key change restrictions), tonally and, by its very nature, as an extremely intimate instrument. Therefore, the Tutor must be more than a book of scales and technical exercises. It must also provide a wide-ranging and genuine literature. To achieve this, I drew from four sources.

But firstly, for the purely technical aspect of the book. A small Tutor and accompanying book of 27 studies had been published years ago by a very fine harpist and musician, a nun of Loreto Abbey, Rathfarnham, Dublin, named Mother Attracta Coffey. I had been fortunate in obtaining a few copies of these small books, for they are long out of print … I have included all the Studies and what is relevant from the Tutor, expanding and updating it to bring it into line with modem technical developments.

Of the four sources from which I drew the music, the first was from our great harper-composers of the seventeenth and eighteenth centuries. For what could be a more fitting introduction to our national instrument than the music of Corneilius Lyons, Rory Dall Ó Cahain, Denis Hempson, David Murphy and the great Carolan. I would stress that in such of their compositions that I have arranged, no attempt has been made to set them in the style of the period because, unfortunately, we know so little of the manner in which they played.

The second source has been drawn mainly from the members of our Harp Society, Cairde na Cruite, and I am much indebted to Mercedes Bolger, Gráinne Yeats, Máirín Ní Shé, Róisín Ní Thuama, Anne Crowley, Nancy

Calthorpe and Ruth Mervyn for their contributions. Also I am happy to include settings by the late Miss Annie Townsend, Treasa Ní Chormaic, and Mrs. Mercedes Bolger [mother of Mercedes Bolger].

No book of our music would be complete without a work by Charles Villiers Stanford, Hamilton Harty and Herbert Hughes. This group of com ers, by translating our traditional melodies into an art form, introduced. This group of composers, by translating our traditional melodies into an art form, introduced them to the great music centres of the world. They never wrote for the Irish harp as it was not fashionable in their day, but I have transcribed three of their loveliest songs for it. With this group of composers I include a setting by Carl Hardebec and one by my late father, John F. Larchet.

Finally for the fourth, and last, source of material I looked to our contemporary composers. While the past has provided us with a great heritage of music we must also look to the future. I realized this meant creating a new literature for our instrument… so I wrote, in the name of our harp society, to our composers, commissioning a short work in any one of five forms. I can only describe their heartwarming response and enthusiasm as quite overwhelming, and as a result, our instrument has now a small repertoire of Solo Pieces, Duets, Trios and one piece with String Quartet, besides a number of Songs to one's own accompaniment, which is, of course, the most familiar role of the Irish harp. To my revered fellow musicians Aloys Fleischmann, Brian Boydell, A. J. Potter, Havelock Nelson, Joan Trimble, Seoirse Bodley, Gerard Victory, T. C. Kelly, J. R. Friel, James Wilson, Daniel McNulty, Éamonn Ó Gallchobhair, Edgar Deale, John Kinsella and Cian Ó Éigeartaigh, I offer my sincerest gratitude and admiration.

Prior to releasing "The Irish Harp Book, -- A Tutor and Companion," Sheila Cuthbert prepared this statement for a brochure announcing the forthcoming book. [86]

inspiring collection of authentic Irish music, *The Irish Harp Book* is excellent for use with any style of harp, as well as any other instrument. Long accustomed to depending upon music published for piano or other instruments, harp players enjoy being able share their wealth with other musicians!

Sheila Cuthbert continued as harpist with the RÉSO, later named the Radio Telefis (television) Éireann Symphony Orchestra, where she served from 1967 to 1987. Retired from the symphony, Sheila remains actively involved in Irish music. In the year 2003, representing Ireland as a member of the Board of Directors of the World Harp Congress, Sheila worked with the Irish Host Committee to prepare for the Ninth World Harp Congress, to be held in Dublin in the year 2005.

MARY O'HARA

Mary O'Hara, though known to many as an Irish harpist, was trained first and foremost as a singer, taking up the harp as a secondary pursuit. Miss O'Hara's first voice teacher was Sister Angela Walshe of the Dominican Convent, Sion Hill, Dublin, where she also studied the Irish harp with Máirín Ní Shé, using the harp in the traditional method as accompaniment to her song. Mary O'Hara also studied concert harp with Mercedes Bolger Garvey, who was associated with the Royal Irish Academy of Music in Dublin.

Among the few modern-day artists with the ability to play passages of music on the harp while at the same time singing with beautiful style, Mary O'Hara become legendary in her own time, with a large following and wide influence. Her early life was exceptional, as noted in this excerpt from the notes on a 1977 LP album:

> Mary O'Hara was born in Sligo in the west of Ireland, educated mainly in Dublin where she learned to play the harp. At sixteen, she did her first radio programme and later repre-

sented Ireland in the Celtic Congress in Scotland. More radio programs, an appearance at the prestigious Edinburgh Festival, TV work, and a contract with the Decca Record Company followed. At the age of 20, she had her own BBC TV programme and ... children's TV programme.... During this period she made known to the British television public many of the beautiful but hitherto little-known traditional songs of Ireland and Scotland. Because of her ability to satisfy both the purist and popular taste, her series was received with wide acclaim. [87]

With this beginning, Mary O'Hara went on to perform widely on radio and television, giving far-ranging concert tours and making numerous excellent recordings. [88]

Mary O'Hara's *A Song for Ireland*, a collection of poetry and songs, enhanced with stunning color photographs of Ireland, appeared in 1982. A book of music, Mary O'Hara's *Songs of Ireland*, was published in 1985 by Lyra International Music Company. This collection of songs and lyrics arranged for Irish harp or piano contains twelve musical arrangements by Mary O'Hara, plus the words to some of her best-loved songs such as "Kitty of Coleraine," "The Quiet Land of Erin," "Oro My Little Boat," and "Danny Boy."

Now retired from the harp, Miss O'Hara has taken up other pursuits. After living in Tanzania, East Africa, for some time, Mary O'Hara and her husband, Padraig O'Toole, returned to the British Isles. Mary O'Hara's full story is told elsewhere and the complete listing of her recordings, books, and music collections is readily available. Suffice to say that she is an artist of outstanding importance to the world of the Irish harp and Irish music. The beauty of Mary O'Hara's early songs with harp accompaniment is undeniable; she sang and played the harp at the same time, much in the manner of the ancient harpers, a difficult art that has not been widely achieved since her time.

Derek Bell

The late Derek Bell, famous as the harpist with the Chieftains, as well as being a solo artist with many recordings, was a master harper and composer of Irish music. As a child in Belfast, Derek's first encounter with the harp, which stayed always with him, was seeing Harpo Marx at the movies. At the early age of seven, Derek started composing music. He wrote a concerto for piano and the school orchestra when he was eleven, and as a youth played his own piano compositions on radio programs for children. Derek won a scholarship in composition to the Royal College of Music in London, and continued with advanced study of both oboe and piano. After passing his exams, Derek was offered a job playing oboe and English horn in the City of Belfast orchestra, and soon found himself manager of the orchestra as well as deputy chorus-master for the Northern Ireland Grand Opera. [89]

About 1960, a harp came into Derek Bell's life in the form of an old Erard harp that needed to be tuned. One thing led to another, and soon Derek was learning to play the harp himself, studying first in Dublin with Sheila Cuthbert and then in London with Gwendolyn Mason, [89] about whom Bell comments in an 1998 interview:

> ... she gave me my earliest lessons. This Welsh lady at least gave me some of the Celtic spirit. 'Til she died, I went to her. I was her last pupil. I was not taught the familiar European method. I was taught a Celtic method of finger placing and all that kind of thing, which differs quite a bit from the French, German, and Russian ideas that are going around today. [90]

Derek Bell applied himself to the harp, studying also classical harp with Artiss de Volt Zacharias and others, working his way through technical concert harp studies such as those by Alfred Holy, John Thomas, and Larivère. Starting in 1965,

FIGURE 34. DEREK BELL, ABOUT 1976.

as well being an oboist with the BBC Northern Ireland Orchestra, Bell became part time harpist for the group. Staying with the BBC orchestra for eleven years, Derek Bell continued his study of oboe, piano, and harp, and cultivated his interest in the music of Ireland.

In an autobiographical article published in 2000, Bell mentions the work he did in the late 1960s with Alan Tongue, a BBC producer: "We researched the old baroque Irish harps with metal braces round the tuning pegs, with horseshoes in each string-hole, and with the whole sound-box carved out of one piece of wood, and strings of brass, played by plucking with the nails."[91] Bell and Tongue worked on arrangements for this harp and in the late 1960s they recorded and broadcast some Irish airs played on brass-strung Irish harp accompanied by a baroque orchestra.

Others, too, were interested in reviving the old harp, among them the noted Irish composer Sean O Riada, who had formed the band Ceoltoiri Chualann, and showed great promise as a serious composer of Irish music before his early death in 1971. His fellow musicians carried on, and in Sean O

Riada's memory a performance was arranged that would include solo Irish harp, baroque string orchestra, and Irish folk instruments. Derek Bell was the harpist and the Chieftains, a group already performing and recording, came with their Irish folk instruments. The featured music for the occasion was "Carolan's Concerto." As Derek put it in his characteristic manner: "Every week thereafter Paddy Moloney asked me to join the boys in a concert." [92]

Paddy Moloney recognized right away what an important addition the harp of Derek Bell would be to the music of the Chieftains. As Bell comments in a 1998 interview in *Harp Column,* Moloney "...wanted to record with it [the brass-strung harp] immediately. He would have even liked to have used it all the time, but I found out that in badly heated halls and overheated halls, it was quite impossible to use the darn thing, because the tuning was not stable." [93] In his work with the Chieftains and on his solo albums, Derek Bell plays various forms of the wire-strung harp, which he calls simply the Irish harp, as well as a nylon-strung neo-Irish or "neo-Celtic" harp.

Being able to play the music of Turlough O'Carolan in a meaningful way is a goal of many harpers and Irish musicians. Derek Bell, the foremost modern interpreter of the music of Carolan, and the Chieftains, have achieved this many times over in their worldwide public performances and their numerous albums. On *Carolan's Receipt,* [94] a 1975 solo album with accompaniment by the Chieftains, Derek Bell brilliantly performs fifteen pieces by the eighteenth-century harper. A second album, *Carolan's Favourite*, followed with thirteen more Carolan pieces played by Bell in the same interpretive style.

✳ ✳ ✳ ✳

Derek Fleetwood Bell died on Thursday, the 17th of October, 2002, while on a performance and recording trip in the United States. Born on October 21, 1935 in Belfast, he would have been sixty-seven years old on his birthday in 2002. Parallel with his exciting career with the Chieftains, Derek Bell had a life-long career in classical music, playing pedal harp, oboe, piano, and flute, with many performances and recordings. In the year 2000, Derek Bell was honored by Queen Elizabeth II at Buckingham Palace, with the title M.B.E. (Member of the British Empire) for his services to Traditional and Classical Music and Composition.

FIGURE 35. DEREK BELL, 1973.

JANET HARBISON

Janet Harbison is a prominent performer and teacher of the Irish harp, a composer of music, and a leader in the present revival of the Irish harp in Ireland. Janet's Irish Harp Company offers publications and harp instruction, sponsors concerts and festivals, and organizes a number of Irish harp performing ensembles. A prolific author, Janet was asked in 1980 by Comhaltas Ceoltóirí Éireann to write the chapter on Irish Harp in their manual for evaluating harp competitions. Compositions by Janet Harbison include her 1995 work, the "Ulster Symphony" and the "Columban Suite," an original work that commemorates Saint Columba, the patron of Irish arts in the sixth century. Janet's musical style combines many influences and her works have been recorded for use in television and film productions.

Janet Harbison grew up in Dublin in a home filled with classical music; her father was a classical pianist from a Northern Irish family of music teachers. Janet discovered traditional Irish music as a girl while attending boarding school in the Gaeltacht, the Irish-speaking area of Ireland. Later, in Dublin Janet studied pedal harp and then turned to the Irish harp. With her extensive credentials and accomplishments, Janet has combined her knowledge of classical music with her understanding and appreciation of traditional music-making, helping to bridge some gaps that have existed between the two.

Janet feels that the Irish harp has a special position in regard to the role of music in the troubles of Northern Ireland; the harp represents a shared heritage not necessarily associated with political factions. In 1986, Janet established a summer school for harp students from both Ulster and the Republic in the Donegal village of Glencolumbkille in the north of Ireland. The following year studies in fiddle, flute, tin whistle, and Uilleann pipes were added, drawing many more students. With a purpose beyond making music, Janet continues to work in the direction of peace and reconciliation in Ireland. This excerpt from her biography in the pages of the Irish Harp Company web site explains her view:

> ...perhaps the harp, its music and history might bring young people in Northern Ireland out of their segregated communities ... and by celebrating their mutual heritage, bridges might be built between them. [95]

In the late 1980s, Janet Harbison organized a concert of young Northern Irish harpers as part of a government sponsored music program to help divided communities understand each other's history and culture. The performance was so successful that the group continued under Janet's direction, leading to the founding in 1992 of what came to be

---

Meeting Janet Harbison in 1980

In 1980 Janet Harbison was chosen to be the first Irish harper to be part of a long concert tour through North America by the Irish traditional music society, Comhaltas Ceoltoiri Éireann. We had a branch of this Irish cultural society in Seattle, so my husband and I offered to host some musicians in our home. It was in late October 1980 that the musicians and dancers arrived, bone-weary from the long cross-country trip by bus. Three of the musicians were delivered to our home: Janet, a harper; Treasa, a dancer; and Penny, their manager. You may be sure that Janet and I had lots to talk about, trading harps and news.

The concert in Seattle, with all their fellow musicians and dancers, was delightful, and enjoyed by a large audience. At their departure we drove our visitors to Sea-Tac Airport. Janet carried her harp with her. As we were waiting at the gate for the plane to arrive, Janet suddenly bent down, unpacked her harp, and began to play. It was a song of joy, as well as farewell. That was a long time ago. I knew then that Janet Harbison was a woman who would make a difference in her promising future career.

Some twenty years later now, I have recently been impressed with *Dear Harp of My Country*, a collaboration between Janet Harbison and James Flannery, tenor, who sings while Janet plays Irish harp. I especially enjoyed this album, as Flannery sings the old melodies of Irish poet Thomas Moore, the same music my mother used to sing, accompanying herself on the piano.

--NJC

called the Belfast Harp Orchestra, composed of young harpers from all parts of Ireland. This ensemble performed widely in Ireland that year in connection with a commemoration of the 1792 Belfast Harp Festival, two hundred years earlier. The Belfast Harp Orchestra went on to tour widely, including a world tour in 1993 with The Chieftains, which led to a Grammy award-winning album, *The Celtic Harp.* [96]

In 1999, Janet Harbison assembled many of the original members of the 1992 Belfast Harp Orchestra for a concert tour, resulting in the founding of a professional ensemble, the Irish Harp Orchestra. As a model for other youth orchestras, the Belfast Harp Orchestra continues to train young musicians in Northern Ireland. Janet's future plans include the establishment of an American Irish Harp Orchestra in Milwaukee as well as other ensembles in Ireland. In July of 2002, Janet Harbison and her husband, Malcolm Gullis, established the long-planned Irish Harp Center in Castleconnell, County Limerick, from which Janet's important work continues.

Máire Ní Chathasaigh

Máire Ní Chathasaigh, of County Cork, Ireland, has developed a traditional style of Irish harp playing that has greatly influenced the new generation of harpers in Ireland. From a large traditional music family of singers, fiddlers, and whistle players, Máire was one of the first harpers in this century to play traditional Irish dance music, jigs and reels, again on the harp.

Máire Ní Chathasaigh records, performs, and tours widely, together with guitarist Chris Newman, and in 2001 was awarded the highest possible honor for a traditional musician in Ireland "for the positive influence she has had on the young generation of harpers." More about the work and current recordings of this important artist can be found on the web site of Old Bridge Music.

Gráinne Hambly

Gráinne Hambly from County Mayo in the west of Ireland is among the new generation of harpers in Ireland and has demonstrated her serious purpose by the excellence with which she pursues her art. In the notes to her first solo album, *Between the Showers*, released in 1999, Gráinne states simply that Janet Harbison taught her the harp. In addition she has made a complete study of traditional Irish music, focusing on the harp in 18th-century Ireland and folk music collections of that time. [97] Also a skilled concertina player, Gráinne is a former member and leader of the Belfast Harp Orchestra, and is a member of the Irish National Harp Ensemble.

A new sound can be heard in her music. Nearly half the pieces in a 2002 performance as well as those on her first album are characteristic Irish dance tunes. It is difficult for the harp to do justice to the brisk rhythm of the reels, the more moderate tempo of the jigs, slip jigs, and the slower hornpipes; dancers need the proper tempo for their music or it is not worthy of their skill. Gráinne Hambly can play fast and steady enough for any dancer. Listening to her play, the oft-quoted comments of Giraldus Cambrensis about Irish harp playing in the twelfth century come to mind: "...It is wonderful how in such precipitate rapidity of the fingers the Musical proportions are preserved; and by their art faultless throughout..."

Gráinne Hambly's interpretation of slow airs and songs is also expressive in another, lyrical way. Not necessarily in strict rhythm, her interpretation depends upon the mood of the piece, as in a song. Whether a fast dance piece or Carolan's lovely air, "Eleanor Plunkett," all of Gráinne's music is particularly expressive in its own way. Another appealing aspect of her recordings are the liner notes where she not only documents the tradition of each selection but broadens its meaning by including how she came to learn each piece.

ANN HEYMANN

An American woman, Ann Heymann is a leading harper in the revival of the *cláirseach*, the Irish name for the wire-strung harp that was used in Gaelic lands from ancient times through the 18th century. Ann and her husband, Charlie Heymann, form the duo "Clairseach," and have traveled throughout the United States, Australia, and Europe, particularly in Scotland, Ireland, and Brittany, performing their remarkable music. Ann plays her specially made wire-strung harp, accompanied by Charlie on accordion, bodhran, guitar, and cittern. Charlie also enhances the performance with his expressive singing voice and occasional storytelling.

In a 1995 interview, Ann comments on her style of harp, which she calls the Gaelic harp due to its origins in early Gaelic-speaking lands: "the Gaelic harp has brass wire strings and is played with the fingernails… Neo-Irish harps have gut or nylon strings and are played with the fingerpads. Wire strings ring out for a long time. It's a bright metallic sound, said to sound like bells."[98]

Ann has done extensive research on the technique of the old wire-strung harps; she has studied in detail the original manuscripts of Edward Bunting, basing her books on this and other research. As well as playing the harp with her finger-nails, she rests the harp on her left shoulder, so that her left hand takes the treble in the manner of the old Irish and Scottish harpers. Ann has commented on her use of this method and how through her efforts, she finds what she has been striving for:

> Though music can be coaxed from a wire-strung harp in a variety of ways, my curiosity regarding its ancient voice dictated as authentic an approach to performance as possible — even in matters of no apparent relevance, such as playing with the harp on my left shoulder so the right hand is in the bass. While use of a harp with historically accurate stringing,

string spacing, tuning and tension was obviously necessary, it was only after playing on my left shoulder for some thirty years that I realized the major role this seemingly trivial practice had in determining the idiomatic musical style that now provides an historically viable accompaniment to the chanting of medieval Gaelic poetry. [99]

Ann's first book, *Secrets of the Gaelic Harp* (1989), is widely used as a guide to technique on the wire-strung harp. A condensed version of this publication was released in 1998, titled *A Gaelic Harpers First Tunes*. Ann's third book, *Coupled Hands for Harpers* (2001), introduces new concepts and techniques that can be used with nylon-strung as well as wire-strung harps. It also includes sections on the history and theory of wire-strung harps, as well as eighty-two tune arrangements. The concept of "coupled hands" involves the use of both hands working together to play the melody.

In 2002, Ann performed on a David Kortier replica of the fourteenth century Trinity College Harp, using 18-carat gold

LISTENING TO ANN PLAY

I first met Ann and Charlie Heymann when they performed in Seattle at the Folk Life Festival in the early 1980's. They were on one of their many early tours, dedicated traveling musicians in their quest for an authentic music. I first heard at the time the "bell-like tone" of the wire strings. This sound is very resonant and beautiful.

I have their first recording, *Let Erin Remember*, with the portrait of Ann's remarkable harp made by Jay Witcher on the cover of a 33 1/3 long play record. I also still have my copy of their second LP album, *Ann's Harp*, which I purchased in 1981. On their CD released in 2002, Hèman Dubh, I find the same careful attention to historical documentation and stories about the pieces they play as I noticed when I first heard Ann and Charlie years ago. One set of six pieces on this album, the King James Set, presents in historic detail Ireland's sad story. For example, the piece titled "The Wild Geese" brings to mind the time in the latter part of the 17th century when thousands of Ireland's fighting men and their leaders fled to the Continent forever. This slow air, "The Wild Geese," is a poignant lament for the exiled Irish soldiers, still played wherever harpers meet.

--NJC

141

wire for the bass strings. The first modern player to use gold wire in this way, Ann feels that this is a historically viable practice. Commenting on her future plans, Ann writes, "While the traditions and historical performance practice of the Gaelic harp remain my primary focus, I intend to continue to investigate modern composition and the application of new techniques and other inventions. After all, these are essential elements in a living tradition!" [100]

FIGURE 36. BRASS FIGURINE OF AN IRISH HARPIST.

Philip Boulding

Philip Boulding has been making and playing Celtic harps for many years as part of Magical Strings, the perfomance group he forms together with his wife Pam Boulding, playing hammered dulcimer, and other musicians on occasion. With numerous recordings, the Bouldings have played many compositions by Turlough O'Carolan and other traditional Irish pieces. In later recordings they compose and arrange all their own music, often based on Irish themes.

As a contemporary musician, Philip harkens back to the three moods of music defined centuries ago, those pieces required to be performed by musicians of the highest rank in ancient Éireann: the *suantraighe*, or lullaby; the *goltraighe*, or lament; and the *geantraighe*, showing joy and laughter. Using these moods in his music, Philip Boulding expresses a fourth mood as well, in "Where Dragons Dance," composed and first performed to harp accompaniment in the year 2001.[101]

Where Dragons Dance
by Philip Boulding

The Bards of ancient times sought to espouse
The mystical three moods, meant to arouse
First joy, and then deep sorrow; thus repose—
But what about a fourth? One might propose
Bewilderment! For these perplexing times,
To guide us through the contradicting lines
Of paradox-of-love, and peace, and hate,
And conflict driving mankind's fate…

If Muses could but seek to part the veil
Of hidden worlds, that shroud the serpent's tail
Entwined in every striving human heart,
Then love-redeeming power might impart
A vision of a future world to be,
Where dragons dance, and all is harmony!

Epilogue

Ever since Roland L. Robinson saw a Paraguayan harp in a music store in Rio de Janeiro, and got so excited about small harps and the potential for making and playing them that he started a small magazine promoting the idea, the folk harp movement has grown by leaps and bounds. Robinson harkens back to standard sources of information about Irish and Celtic harps when starting the *Folk Harp Journal* in 1973, citing authorities such as R. B. Armstrong and Joan Rimmer for where his readers could go to learn about small harps.

With influences from the Welsh, Breton, and Scottish harp traditions, as well as those of South America and Ireland, gradually the concept of a Folk Harp emerged. In regard to issues of traditional and authentic music styles and instruments versus folk music styles and instruments, Robbie Robinson was encouraging to all. He felt that the folk harp movement should grow through one-to-one teaching and with generosity among its adherents. Toward those who sought to pursue what they felt to be the pure version of a style of harp, Robinson was equally encouraging, provided that insistence on tradition does not prevent innovation and invention. Happily, for all concerned, this is what has occurred. We see folk harp circles where a classically trained musician sits down together with someone who has learned to play by ear; both enjoy the same types of music, played on very different or perhaps very similar styles of small harps.

Beginning in the 1960s and 1970s with individual harpmakers, then blossoming in the 1980s with major developments in the making and playing of small harps, the folk harp movement has grown so widely that at least several books could be written on these series of events, some directly re-

FIGURE 37. FIRST ISSUE OF THE FOLK HARP JOURNAL, JUNE 1973. PARAGUAYAN HARPIST LUIS BORDON PICTURED WITH HIS HARP.

lated to influences of an Irish harp, and many not related to anything Irish at all.

Today Comhaltas Ceoltóirí Éireann has over 400 branches around the world promoting the music, song, dance, and language of Ireland, with events attended annually by over a million people. Cairde na Cruite, certainly a main force in reviving the Irish harp in its native land, holds regular harp festivals in Ireland that attract students from all over the world. Regular sessions are held for harpers of all levels with titles such as "Singing to Harp Accompaniment," "Traditional Ornamentation," "Music of the Harpers," and "Wire Strung Harp Instruction." [102]

In Seattle, Washington, quite a way from Ireland yet somehow a place where the small harp has a large following, the first annual Seattle Folk Harp Symposium was held in the year 2002, featuring artists not from Ireland but certainly with an Irish or Celtic flavor in some of what they do. In the year 2003, Dusty Strings again sponsors this symposium, with another round of workshops with intriguing titles such as "Irish

Ornaments for the Beginner," "Gaelic Harp and Song," and "Irish Harp Left Hand Secrets." [103]

In the year 2005, the Ninth World Harp Congress will be held in Dublin. Featured along with performances of classical pedal harp will be Celtic-harp related performances and exhibits from the countries of Scotland, Wales, and Ireland, and the regions of Brittany, Cornwall, and the Isle of Man.

An instrument that has been called the Irish harp in the nineteenth century, as well as in the first three quarters of the twentieth century, is evolving and changing all the time. The recreation of the wire-strung harp, characteristic of Ireland prior to the 18th century, is certainly the most remarkable development of the late twentieth century Celtic harp.

FIGURE 38. MAP OF THE ORIGINAL CELTIC-LANGUAGE LANDS, ALL PLACES WITH A DISTINCTIVE HARP TRADITION.

Author's Story and Reflections

FIGURE 39. SOME OF THE SMALL HARPS THAT HAVE
BELONGED TO JOAN CLARK. IN THIS 1985 PHOTO, FROM
LEFT: WIRE-STRUNG TRINITY HARP REPLICA, MADE BY
KENNETH BOSTARD IN 1974; 26-STRING CLARK JUN-
IOR OR LAP HARP; 31-STRING CLARK IRISH HARP
WITHOUT STAND, MADE IN 1913; DANIEL QUINN IRISH
HARP, MADE IN 1973 IN DUBLIN; TROUBADOR HARP
BY LYON & HEALY, CHICAGO, MADE IN THE 1960S.

My mother Norah, a native of Ireland, had grown up in Dublin and was an accomplished musician. She used to play the piano and accompany herself singing traditional Irish songs. My parents met in England during World War I. My father, Charles, was an American physician in the service of his country. They were married in 1918, and later when the War was over they moved to the United States and to the far northwest corner of the country to Tacoma, Washington, where I grew up.

My mother had heard of the small, non-pedal harp of olden times and had always wanted to play the harp when she lived in Dublin, but never had the opportunity to do so. When I was about fifteen years old my mother saw an antique pedal harp in the window of a house in Tacoma. She went to the door and asked the elderly sisters who lived there if she could see the harp and ended up buying an antique double-action pedal harp that was close to eighty years old. She paid one hundred dollars for it, which was a lot of money at that time. The harp looked like an old Erard design, with a hexagonal column and sculptured angels around the top of the column; however on the heavy brass plate on the back of the harp was carved the name of the harp-maker: Browne and Buckwell, New York. Although my mother liked to pluck the strings and listen to its tone, it was I who became the harp student. As it happened, Edith Lundgren, a well known harpist, lived in our neighborhood and I was able to begin harp studies with her since I could walk to her home and use her harp.

I was an enthusiastic student and learned my pieces but as time went on I found the harp to be a lonely instrument. It was too big and awkward to take anywhere so it was impossible for me to participate as a harpist in the fine music program at Stadium

High School in Tacoma. My father had a small car he used for his work but it could not have carried my harp. If we wanted to go anywhere we went on the street car or just walked. This was in the late 1930s during the Great Depression.

My harp teacher, Mrs. Lundgren, had a collection of old harps in her house. Among her harps was a Melville Clark Irish Harp which my mother rented for a while to play herself. I played this small harp as well and became acquainted with the Irish harp that my mother had spoken of, a harp without pedals which instead used blades, or levers, to change the pitch of the strings. I had always enjoyed Irish music, and admired the Clark Irish Harp for its beauty and cultural value, but it would be years before I took seriously the idea of playing this harp.

Reading about the Irish harp I learned that this small harp had been associated with Ireland for centuries and as the emblem of the country appeared on all the Irish coins. But I was mystified by the fact that although this harp was much revered in poetry and song and was a favorite design device, it was seldom heard. Why was it mute? Why withered the soul?

* * * *

During the early fifties, I sought in vain to get harp music from Ireland. My uncle Frank, a native of Dublin, wrote to me in despair in 1955. "Believe it or not, and I am ashamed to say it," his letter began, "I cannot procure harp music for you here in Ireland. This lovely instrument has become no more than an empty, meaningless symbol." My uncle reinforced his gloomy opinion with a newspaper article on the same subject. Harps were not made in Ireland any more, they were imported. "Genuine Irish" harps, the article reported, were being made in England and shipped out to meet the rising demand for the instrument in America. Even recordings of Irish harp music, much in demand by tourists in Ireland, were nonexistent. This all caused me to think more seriously about the Irish harp.

My uncle did find some comfort in the pleasure of seeing and hearing concert harpist, Sighle (Sheila) Larchet playing with the Radio Éireann Symphony Orchestra. Another article from the paper my uncle sent out to me the following year reported that harp classes had recently begun in Dublin at the Municipal School of Music under Miss Larchet's instruction. Thirteen pupils were enrolled and both Irish and concert harp were taught.

* * * *

FIGURE 40. SCHOOL CHILDREN PLAYING TROUBADOR HARPS BY LYON & HEALY IN A DEMON-
STRATION PROGRAM AT BRYANT ELEMENTARY, SEATTLE PUBLIC SCHOOLS, 1967.

A few years after graduating from the University of Washington I met Byron
Clark, a Seattle man, and we were married in 1948. My life grew busy with rearing a
family of four children. When our children were all in public school I knew that I had
unfinished business in my life and began to take up my harp study again. I was
fortunate to be able to study privately with a noted harp teacher in Seattle, Lynne
Palmer, who suggested that I return to the University to study music. In mid-life,
then, I took the opportunity to enter the U.W. School of Music, where I continued
studying pedal harp under Lynne Palmer, and later with Pamela Vokolek. My goal
was to become a harp teacher. I was able, with my husband's assistance, to get a
modern Lyon & Healy pedal harp. Eventually I began to play in the U.W. Symphony
Orchestra, something I had not been able to do before because of the difficulty of
transporting this large instrument. Times had changed and the new Meany Theater
was equipped with elevators.

Early in 1966, Lyon and Healy provided twenty-four of their new non-pedal Troubadour Harps for a demonstration teaching project in the Seattle Public Schools. Since

I was familiar with the non-pedal Irish Harp I was chosen as teacher for this project. Lynne Palmer composed all the music we used in the harp classes that were held in four different elementary schools, and she coached us all the way. The program continued for two years, 1966 to1968, leading to a gorgeous concert at the Seattle Opera House that showcased the entire Music and Art Departments of the Seattle Public Schools. The harp ensemble of twenty sixth-grade students, both boys and girls, was accompanied by the All City High School Orchestra in a stunning and original piece, *Prelude and Dance*, composed by Lynne Palmer.

✲ ✲ ✲ ✲

On returning to the University in 1972 to complete my degree, I decided to write my senior thesis about the small harp without pedals that my mother had told me about long ago, the Irish harp. My teachers in the music department were not familiar with this instrument, but they encouraged me in a generous way while I continued studying the pedal harp, playing in U.W. Harp Ensemble under Pamela Vokolek, and pursuing independent study of the Irish harp.

The most convincing aspect of my research, however, was attending the series of lectures on the history of Ireland at the University of Washington, given by Professor Giovanni Costigan. His book, *A History of Modern Ireland*, has an Irish harp on the cover, unstrung. That both troubled me and inspired me. The dedication his book said it all: "To my ancestors both Catholic and Protestant." I might say the same.

✲ ✲ ✲ ✲

I had never been to Ireland, but in the fall of 1973, on hearing of the death of my mother's younger sister, I decided to go to meet elderly relatives, and to seek information about the harp. During that first visit, I had the pleasure of meeting harpist Sheila Larchet Cuthbert, who, as it turned out, had attended the same order of Catholic schools that my mother had gone to so many years ago. Around 1900 my mother and her two sisters were day students at a small Catholic school for girls, Loreto Convent, to which they walked from their home in Kenilworth Square in the Rathgar district of Dublin. Sheila Cuthbert had begun her harp studies at the much larger Loreto Abbey, the main institution of the order, located in the more distant Rathfarnham district. During my visit, Sheila invited me to visit the Loreto Abbey with her. It was very impressive to sense the antiquity of this old church, and to imagine my mother visiting there on special occasions.

FIGURE 41. LORETO ABBEY, RATHFARNHAM, DUBLIN, HAS LONG BE AN INSTI-
TUTION WHERE HARP IS TAUGHT. PHOTO BY JOAN CLARK, 1973.

When I told Sheila about my research on the Irish harp, she mentioned that she had a book soon to be published, on the very same subject. I was astonished, having no idea that someone of her knowledge and experience was already compiling the information I was seeking. When Sheila's unique collection, *The Irish Harp Book, A Tutor and Companion*, appeared two years later, it was a major event for harpists everywhere, and not only for those of us interested in the small Irish harp.

✳ ✳ ✳ ✳

I discovered Derek Bell in the spring of 1975, when, laid up with a broken leg and unable to play my pedal harp, I started listening to a new recording of Irish music, *The Chieftains 4*. This was a fascinating example of Irish Harp, solely instrumental, played expressively and fluently, both solo and in the company of such a jolly lot of musicians as I had never heard before! Here was someone who really knew Carolan, someone who could pronounce for me the actual sounds of Irish instrumental music. I turned to the Clark Irish harp I had in the house and eventually coaxed my small harp to imitate the sounds of the lovely air, "Carrickfergus," and then the lively tune, "Morgan Magan," and even the mysterious "Mná na hÉireann," heard for the first time as Derek played them.

I played some of these tunes at the Northwest Regional Folklife Festival in Seattle in May of 1975 and discovered other devotees of Irish music, right in my own backyard, so to speak! The next winter, 1976, brought *The Chieftains 5*, with Derek Bell's bold Celtic harp featured on the cover, surrounded by the companion Irish traditional instruments. As I listened to the exotic sound of the wire-strung harp accompanying the Uilleann pipes in Rory Dall Ó Catháin's tune, "Give Me Your Hand," I knew there was no turning back. I'd found the source of music for the Irish harp, the instrument my mother had told me of so long ago.

❋ ❋ ❋ ❋

Years later, in 1996, I was shopping at Dusty Strings for some music to play and noticed one of the folk harps nearby. At the time I was using just my Clark Irish Harp, having by that time sold the several other models of smaller harps that I had owned and played over the years. To try out the new music, I sat down at the nearby harp and started to play. I was amazed at the sound I heard, at first thinking that the arrangement I was using must be exceptional, then I realized that it was the harp making all the difference. I wasn't even looking for a harp at the time but I bought this one on the spot! The tone was wonderful, richer and more substantial than I had found in other lever harps. After my years of playing the pedal harp, and from experimenting with many types of smaller harps, finding my 36-string Folk Harp at Dusty Strings brought me full circle. This would be my Irish harp from now on. What would make my harp Irish would be the music I would play upon it.

FIGURE 42. MY FAVORITE HARP: 36-STRING FOLK HARP FROM DUSTY STRINGS (FH36) - NJC.

Appendix
Selected Harps and Harpmakers
Some Players of Small Harps
Contemporary Composers
for Celtic Harp

FIGURE 43. COIN USED IN IRELAND FROM 1928 TO 1937.
THE LEGEND *SAORSTAT EIREANN* MEANS IRISH FREE
STATE IN THE IRISH LANGUAGE; THE IMAGE IS THE
TRINITY COLLEGE HARP.

FIGURE 44. IRISH EURO COIN, 2002. TRINITY COLLEGE
HARP IS CURRENTLY ON THE BACK OF ALL OF THE IRISH
EURO COINS, AS SHOWN WITH THIS FIVE CENT PIECE.

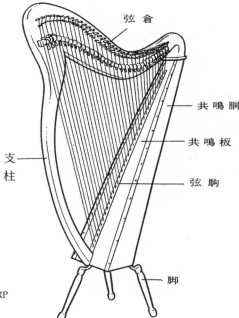

弦 倉

共 鳴 胴

共 鳴 板

弦 駒

支
柱

脚

FIGURE 45. AOYAMA HARP, PICTURED IN THE HARP METHOD I PUBLICATION FROM AOYAMA, 1960S.

AOYAMA IRISH-STYLE HARPS

The Aoyama company was founded in 1897 in Japan to make stringed instruments such as violins and cellos. As part of the family business, Masao Aoyama started making small harps similar to the Clark Irish Harp in the 1960s, a practice continued by Kenzo Aoyama. A harp instruction book titled *Harp Method I* by Tsutomu Mimura explains the basics of the construction, tuning, playing, and fingering style to be used with the Aoyama harp.

A complete method book, this publication includes extensive exercises for right hand, left hand, and both hands, as well as chords, scales, and practice pieces. Masao Aoyama refined the style, and designed his own lever system as an improvement over what was currently in use.

Aoyama harps gained general appeal, and were widely used around the world, particularly in Ireland and the United States in the 1950s and 1960s, when few other harpmakers were producing such instruments.

MELVILLE CLARK IRISH HARP

The Melville Clark Irish harp, modeled after a small portable harp made early in the nineteenth century by John Egan of Dublin, was produced in the United States from 1913 until the 1950s. Melville Clark (1883 - 1953) started playing the harp at age five, later studied pedal harp in Boston and Chicago, as well as in Europe, and performed frequently with both the pedal harp and the Irish harp. After Mr. Clark's death, the company in Syracuse that bore his name continued to produce harps for a while, but eventually dissolved. Lyon & Healy acquired the rights to Clark's business, and produced a natural wood colored version of the Clark harps for a period of time.

In the Clark harp design, a narrow lever or blade is mounted in a metal socket in the neck of the harp beside each string. By rotating the blade one quarter turn, the smooth edge of the blade comes to rest against the upper part of the string, reducing the vibrating length a measured amount and raising the pitch one half-step. Using this blade technique, the harp can be played in many different keys without retuning.

FIGURE 46. STANDARD-SIZE CLARK IRISH HARP AND CLARK JUNIOR LAP HARP.

FIGURE 47. A SIX-YEAR OLD PLAYING THE 31-STRING CLARK IRISH HARP.

The harpist can turn a lever for an occasional accidental during the course of playing, allowing much greater choice of key than had previously been possible.

The harp is carefully made, with crescent-shaped ivory inserts to protect the string holes, and ivory pegs to support the strings. The lower strings are wound wire while the upper strings are made of gut or nylon. A distinctive Celtic interlacing design decorates the soundboard, and garlands of gilt shamrock designs enhance the neck, body, and pillar. The harp is tuned diatonically from E below the bass clef to G, one octave above the treble clef, and uses blades that can be turned to raise the pitch of the strings. Clark harps originally used gut strings, the standard until the 1950s. In 1948, however, Melville Clark pioneered the use of nylon strings for harps, working with Dupont and other companies to perfect the material [1] For a young child, a Clark Irish harp without the stand is the perfect size. With the stand, an older child or adult can either sit at the harp, which can be tilted back, or stand up beside the harp to play. Over the years, these harps have continued to be widely used by both children and adults.

Clark's method book for his harp, *How to Play the Harp*, first published by G. Schirmer in 1932, later reprinted in the 1960s.

WARREN'S WIRE-STRUNG HARP, EARLY 1970S

In 1969, a Dublin clergyman, Rev. Christopher Warren, influenced by Sean O Riada's efforts and his interest in finding the true harp of Ireland, set out to re-create the massive one-piece soundbox of the more ancient harp. After much research, including a careful study of drawings by Edward Bunting, Mr. Warren succeeded in making a replica of the Trinity College Harp, handcrafted of willow with fine brass wire strings. Warren made available an account of how he came to construct his harp, along with an offer of plans for the harp. This work stimulated harp-makers around the world, including Roland L. Robinson, who published Mr. Warren's story and his plans in an early issue of the *Folk Harp Journal* (December 1974). Robinson, eager to publish harp plans and designs, had the previous year printed his own detailed plans for creating a 36-inch "Irish Harp" in the pages of his new magazine. That design, originally appearing in Vol. 4 of the *Folk Harp Journal* (1974) and recently reprinted in Vol. 17 (1998), had lines similar to that of the Clark Irish Harp, including the base stand. Warren's harp, however, was built very differently and Robinson must have recognized the importance of this effort.

In several articles, Warren tells how he found a large old willow tree to cut down, let the wood season for six months, and then hollowed out the soundbox. The neck and pillar were crafted from cut slabs of walnut. Warren tuned this harp in the key of

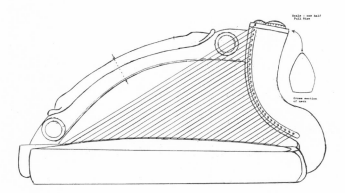

FIGURE 48. SKETCH BY C.B. WARREN, "A MEDIAEVAL IRISH HARP" RESTING IN THE STYLE OF THE HISTORICAL HARPERS. 1974.

FIGURE 49. HARP BY KEN BOSTARD MADE FOR JOAN CLARK IN 1973, FROM WARREN PLANS. WIRE-STRUNG, 32 INCHES TALL.

G major according to the scale as recorded by Edward Bunting (see diagram on page 93 in chapter 7). He played the melody with the fingernails of the left hand and the bass strings with the right hand. Warren's harp had no blades or hooks, and occasional accidentals could be made by stretching the low-tension brass strings. Pressing down on the limber soundboard near the bottom of a string would stretch the string enough to raise the pitch. [2]

While in Dublin in 1973, I was able to meet Mr. Warren and hear him play the harp he had recently built. Played with the fingernails, it did indeed have a rare bell-like tone quite unlike that of any harp I had heard before. I was interested in the detailed plans by Mr. Warren, so back in Seattle I asked a local luthier, Kenneth Bostard, to make me such a harp. Modeled on Warren's plans, Ken Bostard created a beautiful instrument, handsomely hand carved.

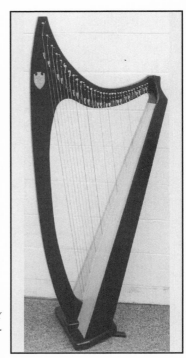

FIGURE 50. TROUBADOUR HARP, ORIGINAL DESIGN BY SAMUEL PRATT, MADE BY LYON & HEALY IN 1969. HIGH-HEADED HARP STANDS NEARLY FIVE FEET TALL.

LYON & HEALY TROUBADOUR HARP

Around 1962 Lyon & Healy introduced the Troubadour Harp, a new design for a small harp with no pedals, using levers to change the pitch of the strings. Originally marketed as a harp for children and beginning players, the new harp was made available by Lyon & Healy for demonstration projects to teach harp in elementary schools. Used by experienced players as well, by 1969 the American Harp Society included a category for "Troubadour or Irish Harp" in their national competetition awards. [3]

The style of the Troubadour Harp has some characteristics of what is known as the Gothic harp, as well as those of the Irish and Scottish high-headed harps. Its name suggests the influence of harps that may have been used by medieval poets and musicians, the French *trouvères*, or troubadours. However, the Troubadour Harp is not a traditional or historic harp; it is a new design that was originally developed over several years by Samuel O. Pratt, a harp designer and manager at Lyon & Healy's Los Angeles and Chicago locations from the 1950s to the 1970s.[4] Although not the first lever harp produced by Lyon & Healy, the Troubadour Harp has been refined over the years to become a popular and widely used harp.[5]

Dusty Strings Folk Harps

Dusty Strings, of Seattle, Washington is widely known as the maker of very fine folk harps. Founded in 1978 by Ray Mooers to produce hammered dulcimers, in 1984 Ray started creating folk harps. Though perhaps inspired in some way by historical and traditional harps of Celtic origin, folk harps made by Dusty Strings, along with those by many other current-day makers of small harps, are original and essentially new types of harps.

Dusty Strings harps are available in three sizes: 26-string, 32-string, and 36-string models are each made of several different hardwoods. The 26-string harp standing on the floor can easily be played by a child, or for adults the harp can be raised, fixed to a stand. The 32-string harp, pictured here, is a compact mid-size harp, easy to carry around.

FIGURE 51. DUSTY STRINGS FOLK HARP, 32-STRINGS, ABOUT 50 INCHS TALL, MODEL "FH32B," IN WALNUT.

OTHER HARPMAKERS

David Kortier, a professional harpmaker for many years in Duluth, Minnesota, built a replica of the Trinity College Harp for Ann Heymann. Detailed photos of the entire process, from the raw willow log to the picture of Ann and Charlie Heymann stringing their new harp, can be seen on his website. In another photo essay Kortier describes a trip he took with the Heymanns to visit the original Trinity College harp in Dublin. His web article "Trip to Ireland (January 2002)" describes how they were allowed to handle this harp, the national treasure of Ireland. He also explains that many of the museum's other harps have come out of storage for public viewing, including, as he states: "the Kildare harp, the Mullagh Mast harp, the so-called Carolan harp, (which Ann calls the Rose Mooney harp), the Sirr harp, and the Dalway fragments, now called the Cloyne harp." Kortier's articles and photos can be seen at http://www.kortier.com.

Since the 1970s, **Jay Witcher** has been creating beautiful replicas of the historical harps of Ireland and Scotland. Included among these are copies of the Trinity College harp, the Lamont harp, the Sirr harp, and the Dalway harp (reconstructed from fragments). Another reconstructed historical harp that Witcher had copied is the Ballinderry harp, fragments of which were found in an Irish bog. All of these models are hand crafted using maple wood and wire-strung with brass strings. For a historical overview, images of many of Jay Witcher's historic harp models can be seen at http://www.harpanddragon.com/witcher.htm.

There are hundreds of other excellent harpmakers and crafters of small, non-pedal or lever harps, both nylon and wire-strung, that could be mentioned. A short list might include: **Clive Morely Harps** in England, run by a family that has been involved in harpmaking since the late 1800s; **Camac Harps** of France, making excellent non-pedal harps that are imported and distributed across the United States; **Thormahlen Harps** of Corvallis, Oregon where Dave Thormahlen has been designing and crafting beautiful, high-headed lever harps since 1984; and **Triplett Harps** of San Luis Obisbo, California, where Steve Triplett made guitars and mandolins before making his first harp in 1982 to fill a local need for folk harps. There are many many more, all over the United States and internationally. For a more information about makers of small harps, see the web page of the *International Society of Folk Harpers and Craftsmen* (ISFHC) at http://www.folkharpsociety.org.

SOME PLAYERS OF SMALL HARPS

Patrick Ball, originally from California, traveled to Ireland where he fell in love with the Irish oral tradition and its distinctive history, language, and music—in particular the Celtic harp. Patrick performs on the brass-strung harp, traveling widely with his Irish-inspired music and his dramatic style as a storyteller. His performance piece, *O'Carolan's Farewell to Music*, has played sucessfully across the country since 1997.

Pamela Bruner is a singer and songwriter, a lifetime musician, who took up the Celtic harp in the 1990s and found her true musical calling, singing to her own harp accompaniment, as is customary for Irish harpists.

Alison Kinnard, an accomplished Scottish harpist, teacher, and performer, collaborates with Ann Heymann on the study of the Gaelic harp, and is co-author of *Tree of Strings*, the important 1992 study of the history of the harp in Scotland.

Violaine Mayor, a player of the historical Breton wire-strung harp, has several albums, including *Dans Avec Les Fees*. She is involved in the organization Hent Telenn Breizh ("The Path of the Breton Harp"), working for the development of the wire-strung harp in Brittany to reintegrate the harp into Breton music. Violaine Mayor, working with Ann Heymann, teaches classes in wire-strung harp technique in Brittany. [6]

Laurie Riley, an active performer and harp teacher, plays at least three types of Celtic harps, and has recorded a variety of music, including her own compositions, on her numerous albums of harp music. As a Certified Music Practitioner with her home base in Sedona, Arizona, Laurie is a pioneer in using the harp in healing music. In January of 2003 Laurie Reily had the honor of joining the Chieftains onstage during their concert in Phoenix, Arizona. In a tribute to the late Derek Bell, Laurie stood in for the irreplaceable Derek, lending her harp to the sound of the band during their first United States tour without their much-missed and well-loved harper. [7]

Kim Robertson, originally from Wisconsin and classically trained on piano, concert harp and voice, discovered Celtic harp in the mid 1970s, and went on to become one of the best known recording artists in Celtic and Folk harp music today. With her engaging performance style, Kim Robertson helped popularize the folk harp in the 1980s, and has contributed a large collection of music books and recordings to the harp world.

Alan Stivell, who began playing the wire-strung Breton harp as a youth in the 1950s, released a groundbreaking album in 1971, *Renaissance de la Harpe Celtique*. As one reviewer notes, the album was a "lush and mystical fantasy that took the world by surprise, and ultimately, by storm." [8] Stivell, an important folklorist, harpist, piper, and singer-composer, contines to innovate, with some of his later work involving a fusion of Celtic and rock music.

Harper Tasche, a dynamic innovator in the revival of the cross-strung harp, occasionally includes Irish pieces in his wide repetoire. On his 2000 album, *Powers That Be*, there is the graceful piece "Lady Dillon," an Irish melody composed and played by Turlough O'Carolan sometime in the early eighteenth century. [9]

Sylvia Woods, of California, studied the pedal harp but her main work began with the purchase of a Celtic harp. She became well known when she began to arrange music for the Celtic or Folk harp in 1978; her first publication is her most famous one: *Teach Yourself to Play the Folk Harp.* In 1980 Sylvia Woods won a major harp award in Ireland at the Fleadh Cheoil na hEireann held in Buncrana, County Donegal. She is known world-wide for her harp business, Sylvia Woods Harp Center, in Glendale, California.

CONTEMPORARY COMPOSERS FOR CELTIC HARP

Almost all of the performers and artists mentioned in these pages do some composing and arranging of the music that they play on their harps. Players of non-pedal or lever harps, like all musicians, prefer to use arrangements specifically designed for their instrument. With the large variety of styles, sizes, and models of these harps, finding appropriate music prepared and ready to play can be a challenge. Since about 1980, much has been published in the way of music for these different types of harps but before that almost nothing was available. Part of the reason for this can be traced to the fact that the modern piano emerged as a major influence in European music at about the same time the pedal harp was being developed. Music was composed and written down to be played on the piano, with its many sharps and flats, and then adapted to the pedal harp, which was designed to play this same type of music along with its sharps and flats.

Historical harpers, of course, had no need for written music—composing was done by ear, and music was learned by ear. But when music for harp began to be written down, it was for the most part music that been created for piano or orchestral arrangement. When the modern non-pedal or lever harp came into use, certain types of music were available only as arranged for pedal harp, guitar, and other stringed instruments; such pieces had to be transposed for use on a lever harp. The lack of music written specifically for non-pedal harps in the first place has contributed to the design of complicated and varied lever harp designs, and to extra efforts required for tuning and playing such harps. These days, many teachers and performers emphasize playing the harp by ear, a tried and true method, and a useful solution to the issue of finding suitable harp music.

The composing of music specifically for the Celtic-style harp is being pursued by some serious composers today, who create and publish significant works, such as an entire suite or series of works. Two talented contemporary composers of music for Celtic harp are Bernard Andres, who is also a composer for classical harp, and Jared Denhard who creates compositions based on Celtic legends

Bernard Andres is a professional harpist in France, a composer of various types of music, and a composer for both classical pedal harp and Celtic Harp. In 1974, he composed and had published a suite titled *Dix pieces facile et breves pour Harpe (sans Pedales) ou Harpe Celtique*, that is, "ten short and simple pieces for the non-pedal, or

Celtic harp." His expertise and knowledge of the harp is evident in his music; it is a perfect fit for playing on the lever harp. Mr. Andres composes suites of music and solos in a variety of keys, but includes no accidentals in his compositions for Celtic harp. His pieces are very good for teaching intermediate or advanced Irish harp players, and his style of music appeals to those who play both pedal and non-pedal harps.

Jared Denhard, a unique composer and harpist who combines traditional and contemporary instruments, creates original music for Celtic harp basing his work on classical Celtic literature. In 1997, he composed *Canterbury Suite,* an album influenced by Chaucer's characters in the prologue to the *Canterbury Tales* (14th century). Later albums include one inspired by archetypes of Arthurian legends and *Legend of the Selkie,* recorded in 2000, influenced by the tale of the Selkie, a legendary creature half-human, half-seal. Along with the harp, pipes, and recorders, this work includes synthesizer and voice. Jared Denhard has also authored a number of music books for harp and flute.

Henry VIII Groat - c. 1536

Mary Shilling - 1553

1658 St Patrick's Farthing

George II - Halfpenny - 1760

FIG 52. HARPS ON EARLY IRISH COINS.

Acknowledgements

I'd like to extend thanks to some of the most important people who have helped me with this book:

First, to Sheila Larchet Cuthbert of Dublin, my friend and mentor since 1973. I prize our friendship, Sheila.

To the late Derek F. Bell, of Belfast: Thank you for all the wonderful harp music, Derek.

To my daughter, Sylvia Stauffer, Editor & Publisher, North Creek Press. I never could have done it without you, Sylvia.

To my harp teachers at the University of Washington, Lynne Palmer and Pamela Vokolek: Thank you for your example and support in my study of the harp.

I'd also like to extend special thanks to:

~ Liam Boyle, a native of Belfast, now living in Seattle, our Irish language editor;

~ Gail Barber of Houston, editor of the *American Harp Journal* during the years that my early articles about the Irish Harp were published, 1976-1979;

~ Nadine Bunn, editor of *Folk Harp Journal* all these years, for telling the story of the Folk Harp over and over again;

And, finally, thank-you to all the authors of books about the harp and about Ireland that I have read and studied over the years.

~ NJC

Notes

CHAPTER 1. CELTIC ORIGINS OF THE IRISH HARP, PAGES 19 TO 22.

1. Joan Rimmer, *The Irish Harp* (Cork: The Mercier Press, 1977), p. 10.

2. Proinsias MacCana, *Celtic Mythology* (London: Hamlyn Publishing Group, 1970), p. 31.

3. Jord Cochevelou, LP album notes, *Renaissance de la Harpe Celtique*, 1971.

CHAPTER 2. GLIMPSES OF THE ANCIENT HARP, PAGES 23 TO 34.

4. Vincenzo Galilei, as quoted in Edward Bunting's *A General Collection of Ancient Irish Music* (1796 edition Reprint. Dublin: Waltons, 1969), pp.24 - 25.

5. Rimmer, *The Irish Harp*, p. 22.

6. Rimmer, *The Irish Harp*, p. 22.

7. W. H. Grattan Flood, *The Story of the Harp* (New York: Charles Scribner's Sons, 1905), p. 27

8. Sidney Lanier, editor, *King Arthur and Knights of the Round Table* (New York: Grosset & Dunlap, 1950). p. 166. The story, *Le Morte d'Artur*, was originally written by Sir Thomas Malory in the middle of the 15th century.

9. Giraldus Cambrensis, as translated by Edward Bunting, in the preface to *A General Collection of the Ancient Irish Music.*

CHAPTER 3. HARPERS, DRUIDS, AND THE BARDIC TRADITION, PAGES 37 TO 44

10. Donal O'Sullivan, *Carolan, The Life Times and Music of an Irish Harper, Volume I* (London: Routledge and Kegan Paul Limited, 1958), p. 3-5.

11. Eugene O'Curry, "Of Music and Musical Instruments in Ancient Erinn."

12. Samuel Milligan, "The Oracular Nature of the Early Celtic Harp," *American Harp Journal*, Spring, 1967, pp 12 - 18.

13. Eugene O'Curry as quoted in *The Irish and The Highland Harps* by R.B. Armstrong. (Edinburgh: Douglas, 1904; New York: Praeger, 1970), p. 1 - 2.

14. Thomas Moore, *Moore's Irish Melodies*. Cork: C.F. N., 1972.

15. Thomas Cahill, *How the Irish Saved Civilization* (New York, Nan A. Talese, Doubleday, 1995), p. 183.

16. Cahill, *How the Irish Saved Civilization*, p. 186.

17. MacCana, *Celtic Mythology*, p. 131.

18. Daniel Corkery, *The Hidden Ireland, A Study of Gaelic Munster in the Eighteenth Century* (Dublin, Gill and Macmillan, Ltd., 1924. Reprint. 1977), p. 70.

19. Corkery, *Hidden Ireland*. p. 71.

20. Corkery, *Hidden Ireland*. p. 65.

21. Aogan O Rathaille, Gaelic poetry, Corkery's *Hidden Ireland*, pp 52 - 53.

CHAPTER 4. THE TRINITY COLLEGE HARP AND OTHER TREASURERS, PAGES 45 TO 58.

22. Giovanni Costigan, *The History of Modern Ireland, with a Sketch of Earlier Times* (New York: Pegasus, 1969), p. 33.

23. W. H. Flood, *History of Irish Music*, p 64.

24. Roslyn Rensch, *Harps and Harpists* (Praegar Publishers, New York and London, 1989), p. 116.

25. Arthur O'Neill, "The Memoirs of Arthur O'Neill", as included in O'Sullivan's *Carolan, The Life and Times*, p. 149. O'Neill's memoirs were dictated around 1810 to Thomas Hughes, Bunting's copyist, and compiled from Bunting's manuscripts by O'Sullivan in 1958.

26. Keith Sanger and Allison Kinnard, *Tree of Strings, crann nan teud, a History of the Harp in Scotland*. (Midlothian, Scotland, 1992), p. 64.

27. Edward Bunting, *The Ancient Music of Ireland* (1840 edition), p. 43.

28. "Restoration of the Brian Boru Harp," *Harp News*, a publication of the Northern California Harpists Association, Spring, 1963, page 11.

29. R.B.Armstrong, *Irish and The Highland Harps*, p. 28.

30. R.B.Armstrong, *Irish and The Highland Harps*, p. 33.

31. Derek Bell, "Preface to Volume I, Great Masters of the Irish Harp," written in 1971-72, *Carolan's Receipt, a collection of Carolan's music as recorded by Derek Bell on Claddaugh Records, Ltd., for Irish Harp, Neo Irish Harp, and Tiompán* (New York: Lyra Music Co., 1980).

CHAPTER 5, SUPPRESSION OF THE IRISH, PAGES 59 TO 72

32. Giovanni Costigan, *History of Modern Ireland*, p. 41.

33. Giovanni Costigan, *History of Modern Ireland*, p. 42.

34. W. H. Grattan Flood, *History of Irish Music*, p.106 –107. The English "Pale" was the area controlled by the Anglo-Normans (the English), which by the mid-15th century was only a small strip of land on the east coast of Ireland, including Dublin and the area near it. The bulk of the inhabitants of Ireland were "beyond the Pale."

35. W. H. Grattan Flood, *A History of Irish Music*, p.106.

36. Giovanni Costigan, story of Silken Thomas, *History of Modern Ireland*, p. 8.

37. W. H. Grattan Flood, *History of Irish Music*, p.111.

38. W. H. Grattan Flood, *Story of the Harp*, p. 73. Inner quotes and italics are from Flood, 1905.

39. Donal O'Sullivan, *Carolan, Vol. 1*, p. 5.

40. Poem as included in Costigan, *A History of Modern Ireland*, p. 65.

41. Details on this siege are as follows: "In 1649 the English soldier and statesman Oliver Cromwell landed at Dublin … With his well-disciplined forces,

10,000 men of the New Model army, he stormed Drogheda and put its garrison of 2000 men to the sword." *Encarta 97*: "Ireland from 1650 to 1700."

42. Corkery, *The Hidden Ireland*, p. 38.

CHAPTER 6. TURLOUGH O'CAROLAN PAGES 73 TO 80.

43. Donal O'Sullivan, *Irish Folk Music and Song*, p. 35.

44. Eilean Ni Chuilleanain, "Gaelic Ireland Rediscovered: Courtly and Country Poetry," an essay in *Irish Poets in English*, edited by Sean Lucy, The Mercier Press, Cork and Dublin, 1973.

45. Donal O'Sullivan, *Carolan, Vol. I*, p. 101.

46. Donal O'Sullivan, *Carolan, Vol. I*, p. 105.

47. Derek Bell, from "Preface..." *Carolan's Receipt...*" , p. 1.

CHAPTER 7. THE IRISH HARP DECLINES, ENDURES PAGES 81 TO 96

48. Arthur O'Neill, "Memoirs..." from O'Sullivan's *Carolan*, p. 174.

49. Edward Bunting, *A General Collection of the Ancient Irish Music* (1796 edition), title page.

50. Edward Bunting, *Ancient Music of Ireland*, (1840), p. 73.

51. Bunting, *Ancient Music of Ireland*, (1840), p. 73.

52. Bunting, *Ancient Music of Ireland*, (1840), p. 73.

53. Bunting, *Ancient Music of Ireland*, (1840), p. 76.

54. Bunting, *Ancient Music of Ireland*, (1840), p. 81.

55. Arthur O'Neill, "Memoirs..." from O'Sullivan's *Carolan*. Kate Martin mention, p. 182.

56. Arthur O'Neill, "Memoirs..." from O'Sullivan's *Carolan*. Peggy O'Neill mention, p. 152.

57. Arthur O'Neill, "Memoirs..." from O'Sullivan's *Carolan*. Miss Conway mentioned, p. 168, Miss Ryan mentioned, p. 176.

58. Comment on "harps in plenty" attributed to Denis Hempson is found in Bunting, *Ancient Music of Ireland*, p. 74.

59. Bunting, *Ancient Music of Ireland*, p.75.

60. Joan Rimmer, *The Irish Harp*, p. 66.

61. For a complete discussion of this harp, see Nancy Hurrell, "A Harp from 19th Century Ireland: The Royal Portable Harp by John Egan," *Folk Harp Journal*, No. 119, Spring 2003.

CHAPTER 8. IRISH LOSS, SURVIVAL, AND A NEW SPIRIT, PAGES 97 TO 108

62. Giovanni Costigan, *The History of Modern Ireland*, p. 68.

63. A personal note on this famous place: My mother's parents, Richard and Maggie Kitts, were supporters of the Abbey Theatre in the early years of the

twentieth century, and, with an interest in the arts and music, attended events there during those rebellious years. ~ NJC

64. Chicago Stories, *Network Chicago*: "Francis O'Neill The Police Chief Who Saved Irish Music." <www.networkchicago.com/chicagostories/archive.htm> Accessed Sept 23, 2002.

65. "Treasa Ní Chormaic – Described by Mrs. Bolger as the 'real descendant of the old Harpers.' Her first harp was found in a bog and she was taught to play by her father." Cuthbert, *Irish Harp Book*, p. 237.

66. Excerpt from Una Townshend, niece of Caroline Townshend, as quoted in *George Townshend*, by David Hofman. Oxford: George Ronald Press, 1983, p. 15.

67. Cuthbert, *The Irish Harp Book*, p. 238.

68. Royal Irish Academy Of Music, Irish Harp Examinations, Grades 1-8. <www.morleyharps.com/musicexamirishbody.html> Accessed October 2, 2002.

69. Author's note: This anecdote was related by Patrick Quinn during a visit to the Quinn workshop in Dublin in the fall of 1973. Patrick Quinn had told how his brother John became a harpmaker, shaking his head ruefully while telling how Sister Angela had, as Paddy put it: "pearsecuted my brither, John, until he made her a harp." I was later introduced to the venerable Sister Angela Walshe, by Máirín Ní Shé during this first trip in 1973. I was charmed by Sister Angela's dignified manner and speech, brilliant and twinkling eyes, small and great stature in her white traditional nun's garb. ~ NJC.

70. Brian Cleeve, *W.B. Yeats and the Designing of Ireland's Coinage*, p. 29. Dublin: The Dolmen Press, 1972. The complete story along with the striking images as submitted by all of the seven artists is found in this book.

Chapter 9. Mid-Twentieth Century Revival of the Irish Harp, pages 109 to 116

71. Mary Ellis, "A short history of the Celtic Congress," Proceedings of the 1983 Aberystwyth Congress, <www.evertype.com/celtcong/index.html> Accessed 2002.

72. Jim Seery, "What is Comhaltas Ceoltoiri Eireann?" Jim Seery / Paul Curry Branch. <www.blarneystone.com/comhaltas/cce.htm> Accessed 2002.

73. Some Irish towns continue to hold *An Tóstal* events every year, such as in Drumshanbo, Co. Leitrim, where traditional bands, set dancing workshops, and art competitions for children are featured. In 2001, a week-long fiftieth anniversary festival was held in Drumshanbo. Details from: <www.leitrim.local.ie> ; <www.emigrant.ie>; <www.limerick-leader.ie>. Accessed 2002.

74. "About Us," Cairde na Cruite, <www.harp.net/CnaC/CnaC.htm>. Accessed December 2002.

75. Ronan Nolan, Sean O Riada, 2002. Web page accessed Dec. 12, 2003. <www.iol.ie/~ronolan/index.html> For more information on Sean O Riada, see "What Is Irish Traditional Music?" by Christina Roden <www.rootsworld.com/

celtic/> and the website of The Chieftains, who originally played under O Riada. <members.shaw.ca/chieftains/ Ceoltóiri Cualann-SeanOraida.htm>.

76. Breandan Breathnach, from Foreward to *The Irish Harp Book*, by Sheila Cuthbert, 1975.

CHAPTER 10. PERFORMERS AND PLAYERS OF THE IRISH HARP,
PAGES 117 TO 126

77. Sheila Cuthbert, *The Irish Harp Book*, p. 238. "O'Shea" is a westernized spelling of "Ní Shé" (pronounced Nee hay). Biographical details on are from the Harpist Contributor's section of Cuthbert's book. Note: Irish women frequently use their maiden names, though married. Máirín and Róisín Ní Shé are also known as Máirín Bean Ui Feiriteir and Róisín Bean Ui Thuama. "Ni" preceding the maiden name means "daughter of." "Bean Ui," followed by the husband's surname means, literally, "woman of" or "wife of."

78. Sheila Cuthbert, *Irish Harp Book*, p. 238.

79. Sheila Cuthbert, *Irish Harp Book*, p. 238.

80. "Introduction and Air for Two Harps" (1969), Mercier Press. Commissioned by Cáirde na Cruite. Premiere: Grainne Yeats, Mercedes Bolger. <www.cmc.ie/composers/trimble.html>. Accessed 2002.

81. Mercedes Bolger Garvey's mother, Mrs. Mercedes McGrathBolger, also a musician, first studied violin and piano with Madeleine Larchet (mother of Sheila Cuthbert) at the Royal Irish Academy of Music. The elder Mrs. Bolger became interested in the Irish harp and its history, a study to which both she and her daughter made a large contribution (Source: Cuthbert, pp 237 - 239.)

82. Grainee Yeats, interviewed in *Celtic Women in Music,* edited by Sullivan, Maireid, 1999, pages 240 to 248..

83. Calthorpe's *A Tribute to Carolan, Music for the Irish Harp*, was republished in a full-size edition 1976 by Waltons of Dublin. Calthorpe's books on playing the Irish Harp and her four-volume collection of music for Irish Harp are widely available.

84. Details from a visit by the author to Nancy Calthorpe in Dublin, 1978.

85. Biographical details in this section from personal visits and correspondence with Sheila Cuthbert.

86. From brochure about *The Irish Harp Book*, by Sheila Larchet Cuthbert, 1975. Reprinted here by permission of Sheila Cuthbert.

87. Album cover notes from *Monday, Tuesday – Songs for Children*, by Mary O'Hara, released in 1977 by Emerald Records Ltd.

88. O'Hara's first album was *Songs of Erin* in 1957, followed by *Love Songs of Ireland*, 1958. Her complete discography is widely available.

89. Derek Bell. "How I Came to the Harp or How the Harp and I Came to Each Other," *American Harp Journal*, Winter, 2000, pp. 27 - 29.

90. Anne Roos, "Fire in the Kitchen, an interview with Derek Bell, harpist with the Irish band The Chieftains, *Harp Column*, November/December 1998, Volume 6, Issue 2, p. 9.

91. Derek Bell, "How I Came to the Harp…," *American Harp Journal*, Winter, 2000, p. 29.

92. "Fire in the Kitchen..." Bell interview in *Harp Column*, 1998, page 9.

93. "Fire in the Kitchen..." Bell interview in *Harp Column*, 1998, page 9.

94. Complete title of this album first released as an LP in 1975 is *Carolan's receipt: music by, or attributed to, Carolan, ceol a chum Cearbhallán nó atá luaite leis.* The term "receipt," in lower case, is used here in the Irish sense to mean a recipe in cooking.

95. The Irish Harp Company, "Biographical," article about Janet Harbison, 2001. <https://ssl.utvinternet.com/belfastharps/janetharbison/biographical.htm> Accessed 2003.

96. The Chieftains, with the Belfast Harp Orchestra. *The Celtic Harp.*(BMG Music, 1992). Grammy award for best Folk Music Album of 1993.

97. Gráinne Hambly, Irish Harp, "Background, Teaching, Recordings," <www.grainne.harp.net/grainne.htm> Accessed September 2002.

98. Tom Knapp, "Clairseach: something to harp on, an interview with Ann Heymann," March 1995. <www.rambles.net> Accessed September 2002.

99. Ann Heymann, statement in e-mail communication with North Creek Press, September 2002, used by permission of Ann Heymann.

100. Ann Heymann, e-mail statement, September 2002, used by permission.

101. "Where Dragons Dance," poem copyright 2001 by Philip Boulding, used by permission of Philip Boulding.

EPILOGUE, PAGES 144-146.

102. Cairde na Cruite web pages, <http://www.harp.net/CnaC/CnaC.htm> Accessed December 2002.

103. "First Announcement," *9th World Harp Congress, Dublin 2005,* from Irish Host Committee, 2002.

APPENDIX, PAGES 155 - 168

1. Linda Kaiser,"Birth of the Nylon Harp String, Thank you, Mr. Clark" Folk Harp Journal, No. 113, Fall 2001, p. 43.

2. C.H. Warren, "Building a Mediaeval Irish Harp," "Playing a Mediaeval Irish Harp," and "The Harp that once – could it Again?" *Folk Harp Journal*, Vol. 7, Dec 1974, p 19-20.

3. Printed program, American Harp Society, Sixth National Conference, June 1969. Eastman School of Music, Rochester, New York.

4. Pratt, John W. Details on Samuel Pratt from a statement by John Pratt, September 20, 2002, added to discussion web page titled "L & H Princess Louise

Harp." <www.harpcolumn.com> accessed March 9, 2003. John W. Pratt is currently the maker of "Chamber Harps" in Utah.

5. Lyon & Healy produced a version of the Clark Irish Harp in a natural wood finish for several years, keeping the Celtic decoration as seen on Melville Clark's original harp design. These harps, with serial numbers in the 2000s, included a stand with stronger legs, an improvement over the original design.

6. For more information on Violaine Mayor, see "Ringing Strings," by Dinah LeHoven. *Folk Harp Journal* No. 112, Summer 2001, pp 21 - 22.

7. Laurie Reily, "On Stage with the Chieftains," published in the newsletter *Reigning Harps*, Shoreline, Washington, Spring 2003, p. 5.

8. Christina Roden, from article: "Exploring Other Celtic Destinations," under heading, "Alan Stivell and the Breton Harp." Irish Traditional Music Archive < www.itma.ie> Accessed 2002.

9. For more information on Harper Tasche, see www.harpercrossing.com.

Illustration Credits

Frontispiece: Map of Ireland by Betsy Konzak, 1979.

Figure 1. Cross of Muiredach in yard by Betsy Konzak, 1979.

Figure 2. Map of Pan-Celtic nations by North Creek Press.

Figure 3. Ullard Cross detail by Betsy Konzak, 1979.

Figure 4. North Cross - Detail, Castledermot. Photograph courtesty of the Commission of Public Works in Ireland.

Figure 5. Detail from Cross of Muiredach. Photograph courtesty of the Commission of Public Works in Ireland.

Figure 6. Shrine of St. Moedoc, drawing by Betsy Konzak, 1979.

Figure 7. Detail from drawing of St. Moedoc Shrine by North Creek Press.

Figure 8. Shrine of St. Patrick's Tooth, drawing by Betsy Konzak, 1979.

Figure 9. Trinity College Harp by Betsy Konzak, 1979.

Figure 10. Queen Mary Harp by Betsy Konzak, 1979.

Figure 11. Lamont Harp by Betsy Konzak, 1979.

Figure 12. Lamont Harp from R.B. Armstrong, in *The Irish and The Highland Harps*, Plate IV.

Figure 13. Dalway Harp. Engraving originally appeared facing the title page in Edward Bunting's *A General Collection of the Ancient Music of Ireland* (1809) edition, and also included in the 1969 edition of Bunting's work published by Waltons, Dublin. Reprinted by permission of Waltons Musical Instruments Galleries Inc., Dublin.

Figure 14. Castle Otway Harp, drawing from Armstrong, *The Irish and The Highland Harps*, p. 28.

Figure 15. Trinity College Harp, Left Hand Side View, engraving by John Kirkwood, from Bunting's *The Ancient Music of Ireland (1840)*, facing page 40. Reprinted by permission of Waltons Musical Instruments Galleries Inc., Dublin.

Figure 16. Henry VIII Harp Groat- H & I, circa 1536. Copyright 2002 by John Stafford-Langan, who writes: "This coin is a groat of Henry VIII's first harp issue. The initial H and I either side of the harp are for Henry and Jane Seymour (his third wife) dating the issue to 1536-7. This issue saw the first use of the harp as a symbol on Irish coins. The legends are : Obverse: *Henric VIII D G R AGLIE Z* (Henry the Eighth by the Grace of God king of England and) Reverse: *France Dominus Hibernie* (France, Lord of Ireland)."

Figure 17. Map by Betsy Konzak, 1979. Revised by North Creek Press, 2003.

Figure 18. Image from Lady Lavery A Series Banknotes, Legal Tender Notes 1928 - 1977, copyright The Central Bank and Financial Services Authority of Ireland (CBFSAI). Used by permission of the CBFSAI, and courtesy of the Irish Paper Money web site <www.irishpapermoney.com>

Figure 19. Harp of Turlough O'Carolan by Betsy Konzak, copyright 1979. A photo of this harp, shown with the strings in disarray as preserved in the museum, appears in Joan Rimmer's *The Irish Harp*, p. 62. Details about the harp from Rimmer, p. 75.

Figure 20. "Carolan's Concerto," from Charles Acton's *Irish Music & Musicians*, page 11.

Figure 21. Bas-relief of Carolan, from photo in W.H.G. Flood's *The Story of the Harp* (1905), facing p. 106. O'Sullivan, in *Carolan*, mentions that this work was "commission by the celebrated Lady Morgan, (1783-1859), the 'Wild Irish Girl'" (p. 116).

Figure 22. "Scale of the Irish Harp," from Edward Bunting's "The Ancient Music of Ireland," 1840 edition, p. 23. Included in the 1969 edition of Bunting's work published by Waltons, Dublin. Reprinted by permission of Waltons Musical Instruments Galleries Inc., Dublin

Figure 23. Egan's Royal Portable Harp, Dorling Kindersley photo. "Harp, types" Microsoft® Encarta® Encyclopedia 2003.

Figure 24. Tara Harp made by James MacFall in 1902. Photograph W. H. Grattan Flood's *The Story of the Harp*, 1905, facing page 152.

Figure 25. Quinn Harp, 1974, photo from author's collection.

Figure 26. Walton "Celtic Harp," from Waltons' "Irish Harps" brochure, 1976.

Figure 27. Melville Clark Irish Harp, 1913, photo from author's collection.

Figure 28. Irish coins, from top, left to right: The halfcrown, a horse (1964); The florin, a salmon (1954); The penny, a hen with chicks (1968); and The Morbiducci Pattern Shilling design (1926). Original images copyright 2002 by John Stafford-Langan. These designs are no longer in use.

Figure 29. Design on the envelope and the stamp for First Day of Issue for "An Tostal" stamp, February 9th, 1953. Stamp features a Fergus O' Brien reproduction of emblem of "An Tostal," showing a traditional Irish harp symbolizing ancient Irish Festivals. <www.irishstampsonline.com> Accessed 2002.

Figure 30: Irish harp students at Sion Hill, Dublin, 1978. Photo by the author.

Figure 31: Máirín Ní Shé playing her McFall Tara harp, 1978. Photo by the author.

Figure 32. Excerpt from *Music for the Irish Harp, A Tribute to O'Carolan* by Nancy Calthorpe, 1969.

Figure 33. Nancy Calthorpe in Dublin, October 1978. Photo by the author.

Figure 34. Derek Bell, about 1976, from souvenir program. Photo courtesy of Macklam / Feldman Managment Inc., managers for The Chieftains.

Figure 35. Derek Bell, 1973. Photo from personal collection of the author, courtesy of Claddagh Records Ltd.

Figure 36. Irish Harpist figurine. Image by North Creek Press.

Figure 37. *Folk Harp Journal*, June 1973 (first issue). Paraguayan harpist Luis Bordon pictured with his harp.

Figure 38. Map of Pan-Celtic nations by North Creek Press.

Figure 39. Five harps. Photo from author's collection.

Figure 40. Children at Bryant Elementary, Seattle, 1967. Photo courtesty of Seattle Public Schools.

Figure 41. Loreto Abbey, Rathfarnham, Dublin, 1973. Photo by the author.

Figure 42. Nora Joan Clark. This photo and that of the author on page 190 copyright 2003 by Fowler Portraits, Edmonds, WA.

Figure 43. Irish Euro 5 cent, 2001. Copyrighted image used by permission of the Department of Finance of the Republic of Ireland.

Figure 44. "The common obverse (1928 to 1937)", copyright 2002 by John Stafford-Langan, who writes of this 1928 design: "The legend *Saorstat Eireann* (Irish Free State, in Irish) surrounds, and the date is divided either side of the harp."

Figure 45. From *Harp Method I, English Text*. Published by Nobuyo Mimura, Nippon Harp Ongakuin, 1962.

Figure 46. Clark Irish harps. Photo from author's collection.

Figure 47. Child playing Clark harp. Photo from author's collection.

Figure 48. Sketch by C.B. Warren, from the *Folk Harp Journal*, Vol. 7, 1974.

Figure 49. Bostard harp. Photo from author's collection.

Figure 50. Troubadour harp. Photo from author's collection.

Figure 51. Dusty Strings Folk Harp. Used by permission from Sue Mooers of Dusty Strings.

Figure 52. Early Irish coins. Henry VIII Groat, c. 1536; Mary Shilling, 1553; St. Patrick's Farthing, 1658; George II Halfpenny, 1760. Original images copyright 2002 by John Stafford-Langan. To view a complete history of Irish coins, see his website at http://www.irishcoinage.com.

Ornamented letters on back matter pages are adapted from designs found in the Book of Kells, as shown in *Celtic Art, the Methods of Construction* by George Bain. Dover Publications, 1973.

Drawing of tuning keys on pages 149 and 170 by Anna Bezzo-Clark, used by permission of the artist.

Drawing of Irish coin on the title page and in the watermark design on chapter pages, adapted from a drawing by James R. T. Norquay, used by permission of the artist.

Bibliography

Acton, Charles. *Irish Music & Musicians,* in The Irish Heritage Series. No. 15. Dublin: Eason & Son Ltd, 1978.

Armstrong, Robert. *The Irish and The Highland Harps.* Edinburgh: Douglas, 1904; New York: Praeger, 1970.

Breathnach, Brendán. *Folk Music and Dances of Ireland.* Revised ed. Dublin and Cork: The Mercier Press, 1977.

Bunting, Edward.

> *The Ancient Music of Ireland.* Dublin: Waltons Piano and Musical Instrument Galleries, Ltd., 1969. A compilation of:

>> *A General Collection of the Ancient Irish Music.* Dublin: W. Power & Co., 1796.

>> *Ancient Music of Ireland.* London: Clementi & Co., 1809.

>> *A Collection of The Ancient Music of Ireland.* Dublin: Hodges & Smith, 1840.

Calthorpe, Nancy. *A Tribute to O'Carolan.* Dublin, 1970. Reprint, Dublin: Waltons, 1976.

Cahill, Thomas. *How the Irish Saved Civilization, The Untold Story of Ireland's Heroic Role from the Fall of Rome to the Rise of Medieval Europe.* New York: Nan A. Talese, Doubleday, 1995.

Clark, Nora Joan. "A Renaissance of the Irish Harp" Vol. 4, No. 3 (Winter 1976); "The Irish Harp" Vol. 6, No. 3 (Summer 1978) pp. 3-12; "The Irish Harp – Part II" (Winter 1978); "Contemporary Use of the Irish Harp" Vol. 6, No. 4 (Summer 1979) pp. 31-39. Article series in *American Harp Journal.*

> *Renaissance of the Irish Harp.* Seattle: Harps West, 1979.

> *Renaissance of the Irish Harp.* Houston: Afghan Press, 2000.

Clarsach.net. Numerous articles by those involved in the current-day restoration of ancient harps and current usage of the wire-strung Gaelic harp (www.clarsach.net).

Cleeve, Brian. *W. B. Yeats and the Designing of Ireland's Coinage.* Dublin: The Dolmen Press, 1972.

Cone, Polly, Ed. *Treasurers of Early Irish Art, 1500 B.C. to 1500 A.D, from the Colletions of the National Museum of Ireland, Royal Irish Academy, Trinity College, Dublin.* New York: Metropolitan Museum of Art, 1977.

Corkery, Daniel.

> *The Fortunes of the Irish Language.* Cork: The Mercier Press, 1968.

> *The Hidden Ireland, A Study of Gaelic Munster in the Eighteenth Century.* Dublin: Gill and Macmillan, Ltd., first published 1924, reprinted, 1977.

Costigan, Giovanni. *A History of Modern Ireland, with a Sketch of Earlier Times.* New York: Pegasus, 1969

Cuthbert. Sheila Larchet. *The Irish Harp Book, a Tutor and Companion*. Cork and Dublin: The Mercier Press, 1975.

Flood, W. H. Grattan. *A History of Irish Music*. New York: Praeger Publishers, facsimile edtition by Irish University Press, Shannon, Ireland, 1970. First published in Dublin, 1905.

Flood, W. H. Grattan. *The Story of the Harp*. New York: Charles Scribner's Sons, 1905.

Fox, Charlotte Milligan. *Annals of the Irish Harpers*. London: Smith, Elder & Co., 1911.

   Note: Charlotte M.Fox produced *Annals of the Irish Harp* in 1911, in Belfast, based on documents from Dr. Louis MacRory, grandson of Edward Bunting.

Henry, Françoise. *Irish Art during the Viking Invasions (800 —1020 A.D.)*. Ithaca, New York: Cornell Univeristy Press, 1967.

Henry, Françoise. *Irish Art in the Romanesque Period (1020 —1170 A.D.), Cornell Univeristy Press*, Ithaca, New York. 1970.

Henry, Françoise. *Irish High Crosses*. Dublin: Cultural Relations Committee, 1964.

Hughes, Herbert. *Irish Country Songs*. Volume 1. London: Boosey & Hawkes, 1909.

James, Simon. *The World of the Celts*. London: Thames and Hudson, 1993.

Kaiser, Linda. "Birth of the Nylon Harp String, Thank you, Mr. Clark" *Folk Harp Journal*, No. 113, Fall 2001, pp. 43-46.

MacCana, Proinsias. *Celtic Mythology*. London: Hamlyn Publishing Group Limited, 1970.

Milligan, Samuel. "The Oracular Nature of the Early Celtic Harp", *American Harp Journal*, Spring, 1967.

Mimura, Tsutomu, editor. *Harp Method I, English Text*. Published by Nobuyo Mimura, Nippon Harp Ongakuin, 1962.

Moore, Thomas. *Moore's Irish Melodies*. Cork: C.F. N., 1972.

O'Curry, Eugene. "Of Music and Musical Instruments in ancient Erinn," Lecture #30 in *Lectures on the Manners and Customs of the Ancient Irish*, edited by W. K. Sullivan. Dublin, 1873.

   Note: The O'Curry lecture series were delivered at the Catholic University of Ireland in 1855.

O'Sullivan, Donal. *Carolan, The Life Times and Music of an Irish Harper, Volume I* and *Volume II*. London: Routledge and Kegan Paul Limited, 1958. Note: Comprehensive source on Turlough O'Carolan. Volume I describes the times in which Carolan lived, including much of Carolan's poetry and 120 pages of his music. Volume II contains the "Notes to the Tunes" and the "Memoirs of Arthur O'Neill."

O'Sullivan, Donal. *Irish Folk Music and Song*. Dublin: Sign of the Three Candles. 1952.

O'Sullivan, Donal, *Songs of the Irish*. Dublin: The Mercier Press, 1981.

Porter, Arthur Kingsley. *The Crosses and Culture of Ireland*. New Haven: Yale University Press, 1931.

Raftery, Dr. Joseph. *The Celts*. Dublin and Cork: The Mercier Press, 1964.

Rensch, Roslyn. *The Harp, Its History, Technique and Repertoire*. New York: Praeger, 1969.

Rensch, Roslyn. *Harps and Harpists*. New York: Praeger, 1989.

Rensch-Erbes, Roslyn, "Harp Carvings on the Irish Crosses," *American Harp Journal*, Winter, 1974.

Rimmer, Joan. *The Irish Harp, Cláirseach nahÉireann*. In Irish Life and Culture Series, Vol. XVI. Dublin: The Mercier Press, 1977.

Sanger, Keith and Kinnard, Alison, *Tree of Strings, crann nan teud, a History of the Harp in Scotland*. Midlothian, Scotland, 1992.

Sullivan, Maireid. *Celtic Women*. Kingston, Ontario: Quarry Press, 1999.

Went, Dr. A.E. J. *Irish Coins and Medals*. The Irish Heritage Series: Vol. 4. Dublin: Eason & Son Ltd, 1978.

Yeats, Grainne. *The Harp of Ireland, The Belfast Harper's Festival, 1792 and the Saving of Ireland's Harp Music by Edward Bunting*. Dublin: Dalkey Co., 1992.

INDEX

ABOUT THE AUTHOR

Nora Joan Clark has written a number of articles about the history of the Irish harp and it's influence in the Pacific NorthWest, where she lives. For many years she produced a newsletter, *Harps West*, and contributed many of these articles to the *Folk Harp Journal*. She also contributed four articles on the history and occurrence of the Irish Harp to the *American Harp Journal* in the 1970s. Her first book, *Renaissance of the Irish Harp* (1979), has appeared in several editions.

Mrs. Clark's formal education includes a B.S.(1946) and later a B.A.(1975), both from the University of Washington. The later degree included three years in the School of Music curriculum with study of the pedal harp. After teaching the new Lyon & Healy Troubadour non-pedal harp in a pilot program in the Seattle Public Schools from 1966-68, she returned to the University in General Studies to follow a course of independent study on the history and use of the Irish Harp, during which she produced a thesis, *The Irish Harp*.

Currently Joan Clark lives in Edmonds, Washington, with her husband Byron Clark and continues as a teacher of Irish and Folk Harp. A daughter and three sons live nearby, some with grown children of their own. Mrs. Clark's study and writing about the Irish Harp has been a personal dedication.

This book is set in Palatino with headings in
Palatino Small Caps and AT Uncial. Book
design by North Creek Press. Printed at
Sheridan Books, Ann Arbor.

Single copies of *The Story of the Irish Harp* are available by mail order for $21.95, plus $3.00 a copy for shipping. For books shipped to Washington state, please add sales tax of 8 %. Send orders or inquires to northcreekpress@hotmail.com, or to:

North Creek Press
~~PO Box 6695~~
~~Lynnwood, WA 98036~~

northcreekpress @ gmail.com

Enjoy –

SB

North Creek Press